novum pro

Oyeniyi Osundina

The Story of Nigeria's Petroleum Industry

1906 to 2013

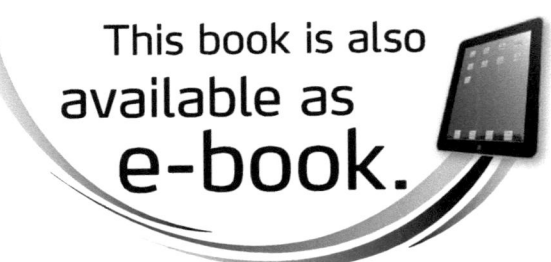

www.novum-publishing.co.uk

All rights of distribution, including film, radio, television, photomechanical reproduction, sound carrier, electronic media and reprint in extracts, are reserved.

Printed in the European Union, using environmentally-friendly, chlorine-free and acid-free paper.

© 2016 novum publishing

ISBN 978-3-99048-204-9
Editor: Chennai Publishing
Cover photo:
Khunaspix | Dreamstime.com
Cover design, layout & typesetting:
novum publishing

www.novum-publishing.co.uk

CONTENT

Preamble 9
Acknowledgments 11
Abbreviations and Acronyms 13
Chapter 1
   Nigeria's Development Dilemma 15
Chapter 2
   Before Oloibiri 23
Chapter 3
   The Civil War 35
Chapter 4
   When OPEC Came 39
Chapter 5
   Regulatory Instruments and Practices 44
Chapter 6
   Leases and Licences 48
Chapter 7
   Participation Agreements 54
Chapter 8
   Joint Venture Arrangements 56
Chapter 9
   Exploration and Production Contracts 59
Chapter 10
   The Trouble with NNPC 62
Chapter 11
   Oil Refining 66
Chapter 12
   Operators in the Industry 71
Chapter 13
   A Comparative Picture of the Oil Companies 86

Chapter 14
    Production Outlook 88
Chapter 15
    The Natural Gas Question 94
Chapter 16
    Petroleum Technology Development Fund (PTDF) . . . 105
Chapter 17
    Nigerian Content Development 108
Chapter 18
    The Reform Agenda 113
Chapter 19
    The Cost of Sabotage 119
Chapter 20
    Environmental Consequences 125
Chapter 21
    Triumph of Failure 128
Chapter 22
    As If There is No Future … 133
Bibliography 150

This book is dedicated to Professor 'Wole Soyinka'.
He is a great source of inspiration
to all who are in search of freedom and justice.
He is a model for those who love dedication
to the ideals of good governance.
Throughout his life,
he has made full use of his endowments,
even in the face of all obstacles,
to fight injustice and corruption.
He has demonstrated that we are capable of pursuing
even uncommon goals and leave imprints.

PREAMBLE

Writing a book anywhere is not an easy adventure. Those who write as a calling will confirm this. Writing a book in the Nigerian environment is a very difficult ambition indeed. But, choosing to write a book on the oil and gas industry of Nigeria is confronted by many frustrations. The first problem is facing research in the Nigerian environment is the dearth of literature. I tried to scout for literature on the subject in our university libraries, research libraries and even the NNPC library, with no dicer at all.

The petroleum industry in Nigeria was born in 1956, prior to independence, but the actual exploration of petroleum products dates back to the start of the 20th century (about 1906, during colonial rule). Literature on the early years was inclusively created by the colonial office, through the organs of the colonial administration in Lagos and London.

There is no library in Nigeria in which one could find the complete record of activities of the period, from 1906 to 1960, for the purpose of capturing the story of Nigeria's oil and gas Industry. Relying only on what could be found in Nigeria would have amounted to doing a story without a foundation or doing no story at all. The National Archives and the British Library in London provided my total needs in the form of documents, correspondences and ordinances/acts of the colonial administration. The British Library provided ample literature on activities, reports and analyses on the petroleum industry throughout the globe.

I decided not to interview anybody because enough factual information was available from the two institutions. The other reason for not interviewing people was to avoid contentious personal opinions, since we all know that controversies surround the governance of the petroleum industry in Nigeria. I wanted to document the history of the industry from its inception to June 2012.

Whatever conclusions I have reached in the project are not mine, but the observations of organizations, institutions and the governments who have stakes in the industry, or who are engaged in the study and monitoring of the sector around the world. I do not claim that this book is a complete account, nor is it a perfect documentation of all the events from 1906 till date. Attempting to achieve that would have resulted in a book too massive to read. My goal was to put together a readable book, which traces the journey from the beginning, using only what I consider to be of value, drawing heavily from what has been stated by law, policy, in operations and in terms of the pronouncements of the stakeholders in the industry at various stages.

ACKNOWLEDGMENTS

I am greatly indebted to the National Archives and the British Library in London for the opportunity to consult their collections unimpeded. On my first exploratory visit to the National Archives in London, my inspiration increased sharply as a result of the richness of their collection on this subject. The first search of their catalogue was made very easy by one of the ladies on the users' services desk, who took great pains to lecture me on how to explore the catalogue. I regret not knowing the name of the lady. I enjoyed every minute of my time, because the service on the first floor was exactly what I needed. I am grateful to the staff who retrieved the documents I requested for.

I am heavily indebted to the British Library where I had access to past and current literature. It is amazing how the staff and management in the library cope with the diversity of the needs of researchers with maximum dedication. Even items requested which were not on site were procured for readers from other locations outside London. I had carried out research for two previous books using the British Library, and I can vouch for the exemplary conduct and supportive role of the staff. I am deeply grateful to all the staff of the Business and IP Centre, Social Science Floor and the Humanities Reading room.

I acknowledge the copious work done by Business Monitor International, publishers of the Oil and Gas Report, a quarterly publication on which I relied heavily for information. The currency of their work and analysis were very useful. I am grateful for their contribution.

The Institute of Development Studies in Brighton provided me with the launching pad for this book. The IDS was my host for several weeks during my literature search. I am grateful for their support.

This acknowledgment would be incomplete if I do not mention my younger brother, Adebodun, who generously offered one of his bedrooms in London which he converted to a study for me to work whenever I returned from my research work. It was his offer that spared me the cost of hotel bills. His act is an unforgettable contribution to my work, he is a brother indeed.

I am very grateful to Wale Adejumo, who worked diligently to typeset my manuscript with patience. I am very grateful to my son, Olanipekun, who paid the cost of publishing this book. His generosity is historic. He is a darling son.

ABBREVIATIONS AND ACRONYMS

bbl:	barrel
bcm:	billion cubic metres
b/d:	barrels per day
bn:	billion
boe:	barrels of oil equivalent
EOR:	enhanced oil recovery
EPSA:	exploration and production sharing agreement
FID	final investment decision
FTZ:	free trade zone
GDP	gross domestic product
GTL:	gas-to-liquids
IEA:	International Energy Agency
IOC:	international oil company
Km:	kilometres
LNG:	liquefied natural gas
LPG:	liquefied petroleum gas
m:	metres
mcm:	million cubic metres
mn:	million
MoU:	memorandum of understanding
mt:	metric tone
NGL:	natural gas liquids
NOC:	national oil company
OPEC:	Organization of the Petroleum Exporting Countries
PP:	polypropylene
PSA:	production sharing agreement
PSC:	production sharing contract
SPA	Sale and Purchase Agreement
t/d:	trillion cubic metres

toe: tonnes of oil equivalent
tpa: tonnes per annum
WAGP West African Gas Pipeline

CHAPTER 1
Nigeria's Development Dilemma

When Nigeria attained independence from Great Britain on 1 October 1960, there were high hopes that her political and economic development was sustainable, with a high potential for foreign investment. Obviously, the hope was grounded on the country's great resource endowment, a well-equipped civil service, and Africa's most educated class of graduates. About five decades later, such hopes and expectations have been totally dashed. Political scientists and economists have written endlessly in the search for the reasons and the solutions to the situation. Sadly, the way forward has not been identified, except that the situation has worsened.

Since the emergence of oil as a dominant factor in the country's economy, Nigeria has experienced an agonizing backward movement from promising development prospects to a country with one of the lowest development indicators in the world. This is strange because the promise which oil holds seems to be the very weapon which has brought the country down. Relentlessly, the country's development problem has been fuelled by forces which have remained stronger. There is agreement in all circles, except among the politicians who are the agents of the crisis, that the limitation of leadership is the most easily identifiable cause of the development problem.

Corrupt tendencies have been with mankind since creation, but the tone of corruptive inclinations has attained a pigment which is troubling. In times past, it was uncommon for people to steal from the soup pot of a neighbour, yet pots of soup and food items were never locked up. In those days, community life was built on trust. Treasured personal effects were kept above the ceiling under the roof, where everyone climbed up with a ladder whenever it was necessary to fetch clothes for special occasions. For someone to stealthily climb up to the ceiling store to take items which belonged to someone else would have been considered an abomination, because he would have succeeded in putting his family into utter shame forever. If a man was so perverted that he would, rather than ask for help from his neighbour, decide to steal tubers of yam from the farm of another farmer, he faced permanent ostracism or banishment. Silent barter was a common commercial practice which facilitated trading in farm products in the community. A farmer would put some harvested crops at the roadside post where human traffic was common. The crops were laid out in portions according to units of prices. If one portion of corn was to be sold for one unit of currency, that amount was put near the portion of the unit of currency for the prospective buyers to know. Upon passing by and deciding to buy any product from the post, a buyer collected whatever item he selected and placed the exact amount of money, being the cost of the commodity.

Many scholars and observers saw Nigeria as an emerging country, in terms of its potential for sustainable development. Such optimism was founded on Nigeria's favourable geographical and natural resource endowments. Furthermore, in the early years of independence, Nigeria achieved self-sufficiency in agricultural production, enough for domestic consumption as well as for export. Nigeria also had a large population which could help to accelerate industrialization. These factors continued to make observers believe that Nigeria would be a success story. As if to vindicate the observers, Nigeria experienced an oil boom shortly after independence. That experience lasted for another decade. However, regardless of the potential for rapid development, Nigeria started a downward slide in its development prospects and that slide, rather than abate, has accelerated. After five decades of independence, with an ever-increasing fortune from petroleum earnings, Nigeria remains underdeveloped, with economic and social conditions deteriorating. It is this paradox that I view as failure which has triumphed over the forces of success. What can explain this dismal picture?

A parliamentary system of government was practiced with between 1960 and 1966, when a military coup overthrew the elected government of Tafawa Balewa. The overthrow was masterminded by a group of educated young officers, who thought that failure was gaining a noticeable rise in government. That military intervention led to a succession of military coups which, in the meantime, caused the civil war that lasted from 1967 to 1970. In the interim, the military returned to the barracks after an election in 1979, which brought the government of Shehu Shagari, an experiment with the presidential system of government. Again, that administration was overthrown by the military in 1983, after which Major General Muhammadu Buhari became head of government.

The longest span of military rule came after the sudden overthrow of Buhari's regime by Ibrahim Babangida in August of 1985. That administration was the most spectacular disaster in Nigeria's search for nationhood. It endured for eight years, destroyed the professionalism of the civil service, and monetized every aspect of government, which has become the political and social culture of the country ever since.

The Babangida regime was ignominiously terminated after it annulled the 1993 presidential election results, which Nigerians overwhelmingly accepted as the only truly free and fair election held since independence. An extremely wealthy businessman, MKO Abiola, was elected, but a gang of military officers, with deep arrogance and self-conceited power-mongering instinct, refused to honour the popular choice made by the Nigerian people. A short-lived interim government, led by Ernest Shonekan, was devised, but it was not designed to last long because of the power drunkenness of the military. Sani Abacha took over power as if it was for the good of Nigeria, he implied he was going to restore democracy, but his bizarre and inhuman conduct in government coupled with his totalitarian disposition was probably the worst military regime Nigeria ever had to endure. He died under strange circumstances on 7 June 1998, with General Abdusalami Abubakar becoming the head of state.

In the meantime, MKO Abiola, who had been in detention since 1993, was to be released, but he died mysteriously on 7 July 1998, the purported date of his release. Olusegun Obasanjo was elected as president in 1999, in an election which was perceived to be fraudulent. He was re-elected in 2003, in another largely objectionable election. After eight years of large government with little governance, the most widely condemned election in Nigeria's history was held in 2007, which was characterized by fraud, murder, violence and outright disenfranchisement of the people.

In 1987, Richard Joseph[1] stated in his book, *Democracy and Prebendal Politics in Nigeria*, that politics is fundamentally about the struggle over scarce resources. In Nigeria, however, the state has increasingly become a magnet for all facets of political and economic life, consuming the attention of traders, contractors, builders, farmers, traditional rulers, teachers, as much as that of politicians or politically motivated individuals. Nothing can be truer even today as we now know that in Nigeria, politics is about sharing the 'national cake', not about national interests. Joseph correctly asserted that there is little disputing the fact that individuals at the top of the social hierarchy gain largely from the distribution of state wealth, but we should not overlook the fact that support for such arrangements is generated at all levels. The strength of a nation is the character of its people, whether follower or leader. A people deserve the leaders they get.

Nearly four decades ago, Obafemi Awolowo[2] argued, in one of his famous lectures, that the countries of the world should be divided into two categories economically advanced and economically backward. He was of the view that the use of developing for describing backward countries was a delusion of progress in

---

[1] Richard A. Joseph, Democracy and Prebendal Politics in Nigeria. (Cambridge, Cambridge University Press, 1987).
[2] Obafemi Awolowo, An Analysis of the Basic Causes and Remedies of Economic Backwardness, Faculty of the Social Sciences, University of Ibadan, 1973.

the midst of socio-economic retrogression. Unfortunately, political scientists and economists still insist on the use of the label. Dele Olojede[3], at a public lecture in Lagos, in 2006, said that Nigeria was travelling down on an escalator on which other nations were going up. It is an apt image of Nigeria going the wrong way, while other nations are presumably making progress.

Some writers argue that military rule brought the decline to Nigeria. I doubt if that answers the situation adequately, because I believe that a good military rule may succeed to transform a society, and some countries have been transformed by military rule. Some bad military leaders will draw any nation back and leave a legacy of bad governance. By a tragic stroke of misfortune, Nigeria was ruled, between January 1966 and 1998, except from 1979 to 1983, by a succession of military rulers with no vision.

Oil came, but was used as a weapon against the people. The leaders took the country on a long trek to greed, wealth accumulation, and lack of direction. By the time the military handed over power finally in 1998, the Nigerian economy was prostrate.

Ibrahim Babangida tried to reverse the ride down the speedy escalator by the introduction of the infamous Structural Adjustment Programme (SAP), which nailed Nigeria into a coma. At a point, Babangida told Nigerians that the problems seemed to defy all solutions.

The wounds inflicted by the civil war of 1967 to 1970 have not fully healed today. The misfortune was heightened by the perfection of a form of government thriving on corruption. The new political leadership which was hitherto traditionally unnoticed in politics became noticeable, with the flaunting of ill-gotten wealth and power. That was the beginning of the most obvious syndrome, which Richard Joseph called prebendalism. Prebendalism is the progressive conversion of public offices to serve the interests of public officers, relations, clans, and friends. To capture the long-term consequences of the past scenario, re-

---

3 Dele Olojede, Public Lecture in Lagos, 2006.

call that between 1966 and 2007, Yakubu Gowon ruled for nine years, while Babangida and Obasanjo ruled for eight years, respectively. The succession of bad regimes which led to the entrenchment of the prebendal culture in governance unavoidably led to the emergence of a system of fronting by streetwise men and women, who became agents for the ruling class.

The decline encompassed all spheres of national life, breeding instability, corruption, deception, lawlessness and graft. Ray Ekpu[4] writing in an edition of the Newswatch in 1985 said that in twenty-five years, Nigeria had eight rulers, six of them were from the military, ruling for fifteen years. He also observed that Nigeria had two different constitutions, one parliamentary, the other presidential, but both failed to help Nigeria. It was twenty-five years ago when Ray Ekpu said so. From Tafawa Balewa to the present administration, Nigeria has had five or six constitutions, but the decline has attained a sustained thrust, which seems to be impossible to halt with a political treatment.

When the decline started to show noticeable consequences for the country, Obafemi Awolowo sounded a strident warning, in which he predicted a potential doom for the state of the economy. He was quickly treated, by a federal cabinet member, to a derisive, if not abusive reaction. Awolowo's prediction not only came to pass, his profound analysis is still with Nigeria almost four decades later. The decline which he confidently predicted became a total plague, which has eaten up all the virtues of a nation state.

Twenty-five years ago, Ray Ekpu[5] said that all the ingredients for building a great country were present: land, water, minerals, and human resources. The only ingredient standing between Nigeria and greatness is leadership. It is tragic that his assertion

---

4 Ray Ekpu, The good, the bad and the ugly in twenty-five years. Newswatch, Special Edition, October 1985.
5 Ray Ekpu, Politics and leadership: The end justifies the means. Newswatch, October 1986.

remains a serious factor in Nigeria's efforts to develop. Several scholars have asserted in their works on Nigeria and politics of survival as a nation state that the trouble with Nigeria is simply and squarely a failure of leadership. All concluded that there was nothing basically wrong with the Nigerian character.

Richard Joseph used India and China to illustrate the irony of Nigeria's inability to move forward. In his lecture titled, *Misgovernance and the African Predicament*, presented in 2006, at the University of Ibadan, he observed that while China is an authoritarian single-party regime, India is a democratic multiparty state. While their political systems differ remarkably, both have capable states. Nigeria and India match each other in their degree of cultural multiplicity, but in Nigeria, the state has become weaker, softer, more divided, and more contested generally, being unable to perform the functions of a normal state.

During the first government after independence, the political leadership was not a mindless class. They had legitimate claims to the pre-independence struggle and had noble dreams about Nigeria. Leadership values changed from bad to worse when the fortunes of the country increased in terms of revenue earnings. The question of power-sharing among the regions became pronounced. Mistrust, disaffection, and divisive values expanded beyond the political actors into the ranks of the citizenry. The leadership did not possess the will or the ability to reverse what they were part of. Thus, each successive government, whether military or civilian, was worse than their predecessors. The leaders were sucked in by inordinate ambition, pursuit of self-centred interests, and the thirst for wealth accumulation. The ordinary citizens were easily sucked into the new value system as well, bringing the concept of leadership and followership into utter disrepute.

How are these connected with the intractable problems of the oil and gas industry? First, it was the problem of initial capacity-building, then crass inefficiency, and the scourge that seems to be destroying any hope of development-*corruption*. Therefore, what was thought to bring fortune to Nigeria has brought misfortune. More than fifty years after oil was found in Nigeria, there is little to show for the enormous earnings from the commodity. Instead, poverty and environmental degradation continue to visit the oil-producing communities, while the country has not risen to the challenges of national development in any sector.

The aim of this book is to open a window into the history of the oil and gas industry. Oil brought destruction to the environment, division to the country, and a level of corruption unknown in other oil-producing countries. My desire is not to accentuate the nuisance, but to record what has been happening in the sector. The Nigerian situation is very precarious, especially after five decades of blunder, crises, environmental degradation through gas flaring, sabotage of oil facilities, troubling policy choices, and, of course, lethal corruption. That the oil and gas industry has not matured after more than fifty years is testimony to the problems of national leadership and the failure of capacity-building in the NNPC and the government.

Beyond the sphere of the oil and gas industry, a general atmosphere of frustration is hanging over the country. It seems that the government sees through one prism, while the people of Nigeria see through another. Adaighofua Ojomaikre[6], in an article, said that "notwithstanding the neglect and self-deluding official non-recognition of the massive national adverse economic consequences, Nigeria cannot ignore the troubles". He reflects that "Singapore, Nigeria's former compeer, transited from Third World to first world economy in under thirty years". Nigeria has a higher population, limitless natural resources, far more than Japan, the world's third largest economy. The dilemma of Nigeria's oil and gas industry has become a classic case study because, while other oil-producing nations have learnt lessons from their own experiences and solved their problems, Nigeria appears to be jumping from the frying pan into the fire.

---

6 Adaighofua Ojomaikre, Economy: Undo Jonathan's sealed failure (1) and (2), The Guardian, Nigeria, November 5 & 6, 2011

CHAPTER 2
Before Oloibiri

Colonial office files contain ample records of events which predate the finding of oil in Nigeria. Some of these notes, reports, and exchanges date as far back as 1906. For instance, an article written by T. Hugh Boorman[7] referred to reports made in December 1908 to various companies about the appearance of petroleum oil with an asphalt base in immense quantities on the West Coast of Africa. The Nigeria Bitumen Corporation had attempted to extract the bitumen, but faced great difficulties with transportation. At a meeting of the Nigeria Investment Company held in London at the same time, C.H. Barley Mosley, former colonial secretary of Lagos, told his audience that "I am taking it for granted not only that oil has been found, but that the conditions surrounding this find are of a nature to make it possible to place it on the market in competition with the oils of Russia and America".

Exploration and development work had already been carried out by the Nigeria Investment Company for two years prior to deep drilling. The work confirmed that oil could be found by deep boring and that bitumen could be mined in large quantities and high grade. Also, the directors of the Nigeria Bitumen Corporation reported to its shareholders that "after passing a small show of oil in sand rock, oil was struck at a depth of 633 feet, which rose to within 98 feet of the surface and did not decrease after four days taking. After casing down further and drilling an additional 26 feet, oil increased and production was 145 barrels per day".

At that point, the Rt. Hon. W.S. Churchill, one-time Under Secretary for the colonies, stated that:

---

[7] T. Hugh Boorman, Nigerian oil, English Mineral Journal, 1909; 87: 1037.

"The Colonial Office and its advisers were not mistaken in their prognostications by the development that oil was found in the Western Region, in addition to the bitumen found in 1908, to confirm the view that Southern Nigeria was to become a petroleum producer in the very near future."

Fifty years after that view was presented, oil was found in large quantities in southern Nigeria. A note in the Oil and Petroleum Manual of 1911 reported that the Nigeria Bitumen Corporation had abandoned 1000 square miles in the northern portion of the company's licence, having surrendered 300 square miles in 1910, leaving 700 square miles. By 1912, drilling was in progress in boreholes 5, 9, 10, and 13, and heavy oil had been struck at a depth of about 650 feet.

In 1913, an oil and petroleum manual reported that the Nigeria Bitumen Corporation had secured leases over 3 square miles. In 1914, it was also reported in the manual that the Nigeria Bitumen Corporation had resolved to wind up voluntarily (liquidate) and reconstruct.

The Nigeria Investment Company, which was also registered in February 1906, resolved to liquidate in December 1913. There are file notes showing that a company called Petroleum Lands Ltd. was registered on 25 January 1910, to acquire exclusive oil licences from the southern Nigeria Government, over an area of 420 square miles in the Benin District. The last recorded report on the company was in 1912, after which no mention was ever made of it.

A British Colonial Petroleum Corporation was registered in December 1906 and, in December 1908, acquired a licence from the Nigeria Investment Company to drill for bitumen, petroleum, and mineral oils, over an area of 225 square miles in southern Nigeria. The licence expired, but a new one over an area of 500 square miles between Benin and Escravos rivers was obtained.

Colonial records show that in 1931, one Major E. Seaborn Mark negotiated with the Colonial Office for rights to explore for oil in southern Nigeria, over an area covering approximately 3,300 square miles. Also, by August 1936, file notes from the Colonial Office indicated that communication was in progress between the Anglo-Iranian Oil Company and Anglo-Saxon Petroleum Company on one hand, and the colonial administration on the other, concerning the possibility of obtaining rights to explore for oil in Nigeria. The concession was approved for the Anglo-Saxon Petroleum Company and D'Arcy Exploration Company at the end of 1937.

On 31 December 1937, the companies requested that the licence approved for them should be issued in the name of Shell Overseas Exploration Company, by substituting Shell Overseas Exploration for the name of Anglo-Saxon as the joint licensee with D'Arcy. The request was granted on 13 January 1938.

An oil exploration licence was approved in principle under the Mineral Oils Ordinance (Cap. 94) on 4 November 1938, with the signature of B.H. Bourdillon as governor and J. Humphreys as private secretary. The terminal date of the licence was 31 August 1949.

The first licence in respect of land was likely to have been granted to D'Arcy/Shell Overseas in 1943. Another Submarine Mineral Oil Exploration Licence was under consideration by October 1948. The land licence covered the whole of Nigeria and the Cameroons, while the submarine licence covered the whole of the Nigerian territory. Both gave exclusive rights to the companies. The Mineral Oils Ordinance [1914], chapter 94, subsection 2 of section 6, stated as follows:

"No lease or licence shall be granted except to a British subject or a British Company registered in Great Britain or in a British Colony, having its principal place of business within His Majesty's Dominions, the Chairman and the Managing Director (if any) and the majority of the other Directors of which are British subjects."

In the course of the consideration of the joint application of Shell Overseas Exploration Company and D'Arcy Exploration Company for exclusive rights, there was considerable argument on the question of the application of the Mineral Oils Ordinance, which specifically referred to "lands in Nigeria" without any mention of "submarine oil" deposits for which Shell and D'Arcy also applied. In consequence of the inadequacy of the provision in the ordinance, an amendment was proposed in 1949, to include the areas beneath the territorial waters of Nigeria. During the very many exchanges and meetings between the companies and government on the new licence, it was emerging that the colonial government was wondering how it could secure an interest in the profits from the oil, if it was found in the exploration. This issue was the basis of a meeting held on 28 June 1949, to discuss the policy to be adopted by the government of Nigeria if oil was struck.

As progress seemed to be made on the validation of the oil prospecting licence, the Owerri community raised serious objections to the prospect of the taking over of their land by Shell/D'Arcy for any reason. The Ikeredu Group Council was the voice of the community, with Nnamdi Azikiwe as their lawyer. The misunderstanding on the activities of Shell/D'Arcy in the Eastern Provinces was peacefully resolved.

Prior to the exploration attempts by Anglo-Saxon Oil Exploration Company and D'Arcy Oil Exploration Company, petroleum products were supplied to Nigeria by some foreign companies as contractors. The Petroleum Ordinance of 1889 was concerned mainly with the regulation of the storage and transportation of petroleum products. Organized business in petroleum products was known to have commenced in 1907, when Socony Vacuum Oil Company started to import kerosene to Nigeria. Socony Vacuum Oil Company was the predecessor of Mobil Oil in Nigeria. The kerosene business was purely a commercial enterprise which was limited in scope. Some other contractors involved in the supply of petroleum products included Paterson Zochonis (PZ), Compagnic Française de l'Afrique Occidentale (CFAO), and G.B. Olivant.

Attention began to turn to Nigeria, as oil conglomerates scouted around the world for oil deposits. In order to prepare for an eventual inroad to Nigeria and to take advantage of the possibility of the coming of oil, the Mining Regulation [Oil] Ordinance was enacted in 1909. The Ordinance amended the Mining Regulations, to regulate the right to obtain licence, explore for, and work on oil. This ordinance enabled the Nigeria Bitumen Company (a German-owned company) to obtain a lease to engage in the exploration for bitumen.

The outbreak of the First World War brought an abrupt end to that ambition. Shell/D'Arcy started upstream activities in 1937, but the efforts were interrupted again by the outbreak of the Second World War, which did not allow any action until the late forties.

Upstream activities progressed thereafter, resulting in the discovery of crude oil of commercial value by Shell-BP Petroleum Development Company in 1956 at Oloibiri, in the then Eastern Region. Oloibiri is now in Rivers State of Nigeria. As a result of this development, it was realized that the petroleum affairs unit in the colonial governor general's office was no longer adequately equipped to supervise the emerging oil activities. Thus, a Hydrocarbons Section was established in 1958 within the Ministry of Mines and Power to oversee the functions of the upstream activities. The new section was run within the solid minerals unit.

The growth of the upstream activities continued and new regulations were needed to be able to manage the impending development in the sector. In this regard, the petroleum section was enlarged to become the Petroleum Division of the Ministry of Mines and Power in 1963. By that time, there were six oil marketing companies and nine exploration companies. Nigeria had become an independent nation, and her interests had shifted from taxation to the proper regulation of the industry. That development will be dealt with exhaustively in subsequent chapters.

The table below shows the sequence of the establishment of international oil companies in Nigeria.

Name of Company	Year
Shell Petroleum Development Company	1937
Mobil Producing Nigeria	1955
Chevron Nigeria	
Texaco Overseas Nigeria Petroleum Company	1961
Elf Petroleum Nigeria	1962
Philips Petroleum	1964
Pan Ocean Oil Corporation	1972
Ashland Oil Nigeria	1973
Agip Energy	1979
Statoil Alliance	1992
Esso Exploration and Production	1992
Texaco Outer Shelve Nigeria	1992
Shell Nigeria Exploration and Producing Company	1992
Total Exploration and Production Company	1992
Amoco Corporation	1992
Chevron Exploration and Production Company	1992
Conoco	1992
Abacan	1992

Between 1979 and 1992, ten oil companies entered Nigeria for exploration and production. The period marked the height of intense activities in the oil sector and a time of challenge for the country.

With the increase in the flow of crude oil and the contribution of petroleum to Nigeria's economy, international interest in Nigeria grew tremendously. It became imperative to build the domestic capacity to deal effectively with the newly acquired economic status. In 1963, therefore, the small section devoted to petroleum matters in the mines division of the Ministry of Mines and Power expanded to become a full division, which then became the Department of Petroleum Resources in 1970.

Five years later, in 1975, the department was converted to the Ministry of Petroleum and Energy. From that time, one development led to another as exploration activities intensified. In or-

der to ably monitor and regulate the sector, the government created some agencies to take charge of such responsibilities. Some of the agencies included:
- Petroleum Technology Development Fund (PTDF) in 1973
- Petroleum Training Institute (PTI) in 1972
- Petroleum Equalization Fund (PEF) in 1975
- Revenue Attribution Unit

The petroleum division was originally under the leadership of a chief petroleum engineer, but when the division became the Department of Petroleum Resources, the head became the director of petroleum resources and chairman of Port Harcourt Refinery, who regulated the activities of upstream and downstream companies. The establishment of those institutions was not enough to strengthen the capacity of government to fully control the industry. It was clear that much more would be required. The next decade witnessed the creation of two major organizations, one leading to the birth of the other, which were to become the pivots of the oil and gas activities.

Annex 1: Early British Press Reports on Oil Production in Nigeria

These press reports highlight the interest demonstrated by Britain, which was fully reflected in the British press. The Government Notice No. 2675 in the *Official Gazette* No. 76, Volume 46 of 17 December 1959, is a pointer to the part of a stream of developments occurring in the oil industry, within one year of quantifiable oil find.

Times
28 August 1958: "Nigeria produced 189,325 barrel of crude oil in June and 176,942 barrels in July, 1958".

Birmingham Post
28 August 1958: "Nigeria produced 189,325 barrels of crude oil in June and 176,942 barrels in July 1958".

Times
21 October 1958: The Shell-BP announced that oil had been struck at two wells at Krakrama, Degema Division, and Eburi, Ogoni. Both were drilled to depths approaching 12,000 feet.

Times
27 October 1958: "Shell-BP announced that their exploration oil well at Ethiope in the Delta Province of Western Nigeria has been abandoned as a dry well, after reaching 13,100 feet. The rig was moved to Ubulu in Uku for a new drilling".

Financial Times
30 October 1958: "Another oil well drilled by Shell-BP in Nigeria has been abandoned as a dry well. The well at Ethiope in the Delta Province was the deepest so far drilled in Nigeria".

Financial Times
December 1958: "Shell-BP's drilling programmes at Oloibiri, Nigeria's first oil field, is to be interrupted because of unexpected production problems. The rig was transferred to Bomu in Ogoni Division, near Port Harcourt, where the company discovered oil recently. The company felt that the accumulation of oil was much smaller than originally expected at Oloibiri".

West Africa
Saturday, 9 May 1959: "Interest in their prospects of oil in Nigeria had been quickened by the announcement that Shell-BP hoped that production will reach the rate of 500,000 tons per year by the end of 1959".

Petroleum Times
18 December 1959: "Just six months after being granted its exploration licence in the Western Region of Nigeria, Mobil Exploration Nigeria has struck oil in its test well at Afowo".

Annex 2: A Chronology of Major Petroleum Developments.

1908 Nigeria Bitumen Company and British Colonial Petroleum commenced operations around Okitipupa.
1938 Shell-D'Arcy was granted exploration licence to prospect for oil throughout Nigeria.
1958 Mobil Oil Corporation started operations in Nigeria.
      1956 First successful well drilled by Shell-D'Arcy at Oloibiri.
1956 Shell/D'Arcy changed name to Shell-BP Petroleum Development Company of Nigeria.
1958 First shipment of oil from Nigeria.
1959 Concessional rights extended to other oil companies.
1961 Shell's Bonny Terminal was commissioned. Texaco Overseas started operation in Nigeria.
1962 Elf started operation in Nigeria as Safrap.
1963 Elf discovered Obagi field and Ubata gas field. Gulf Oil started production.
1965 Agip found its first oil at Ebocha.
      Phillips Oil Company started operation in Bendel State
1966 Elf commenced production in Rivers State with 13,000 barrels per day.
1967 Phillips drilled its first well (dry) at Osari-1 Phillips discovered oil at Gilli-Gilli-1.
1968 Mobil Producing Nigeria was formed.
      Gulf's Oil Terminal at Escravos was commissioned.
1969 The Petroleum Act.
1970 Mobil started production from four wells at Idoho field. Agip started production.
      The Department of Petroleum Resources Inspectorate was established.
1971 Nigeria joined the Organization of Petroleum Exporting Countries.
      Mobil's terminal at Qua Iboe was commissioned.
1973 In the First Participation Agreement, the federal government acquired 35 % shares in the oil companies. Ash-

	land started Production Sharing Contract (PSC) with the Nigerian National Oil Corporation (NNOC). Pan Ocean Corporation drilled its first oil well at Ogharefe-1.
1974	The Second Participation Agreement increasing federal government shares to 55 %. Safrap formally changed name to Elf. Ashland's first discovery of oil at Ossu-1.
1975	Agip lifted oil from Brass Terminal. Department of Petroleum Resources was upgraded to a ministry.
1976	Ministry of Petroleum and Energy was renamed Ministry of Petroleum Resources. Pan Ocean started production via Shell-BP's pipeline with 10,800 barrels per day.
1977	The federal government established the Nigerian National Petroleum Corporation (NNPC) by Decree 33 (NNOC and MPR abolished.)
1979	The Third Participation Agreement (through NNPC) increased government equity to 60 %. The Fourth Participation Agreement increased equity held by government to 80 % and Shell to 20 %. BP's shareholding was nationalized. Shell changed its name to Shell Petroleum Development Company of Nigeria (SPDC).
1984	Agreement to consolidate NNPC/Shell joint venture.
1986	Signing of the memorandum of understanding (MoU). 1989 Fifth Participation Agreement (NNPC: 60 %; Shell: 30 %, Elf: 5 %, Agip: 5 %).
1991	Signing of memorandum of understanding and Joint Venture Operating Agreement (JOA).
1993	Production sharing contracts signed with SNEPCO. Sixth Participation Agreement (NNPC: 55 %, Shell: 30 %, Elf: 10 %, Agip: 5 %. Elf's Odudu blend came on-stream.
1995	SNEPCO started drilling first exploration well. NLNG's final investment decision taken.
1999	NLNG's first shipment of gas out of Bonny Terminal.

2000 NPDC/NAOC service contract was signed.
2001 Production started at Okoro offshore field.
2002 New Production contract agreements signed.
The downstream sector was liberalized. NNPC started its retail outlet scheme.
2010 The Nigerian Content Development Act.

Nigeria was a British Colony before oil was found; therefore, the territorial proprietorship of Nigeria's land and sea belonged to the British government. Ample official records in the British National Archives provide information on the activities of the British Foreign Office during the years before independence. The following extracts are listed to provide references to the events from 1931 to 1957:
1. Letter from Major E. Mark, dated 16 June 1931, and exchanges with him.
2. Communication between Anglo-Iranian Oil Company, Anglo-Saxon Petroleum Company and the Colonial Office on rights to explore for oil.
3. The approval for Anglo-Saxon Petroleum Company made in 1937.
4. Request of 31 December 1937, for the substitution of licence with the name of Shell Overseas Exploration Company.
5. The approval of the request on 13 January 1938.
6. An oil exploration licence was approved in principle on 4 November 1938, under the signature of B.H. Bourdillon as the governor.
7. Record of a meeting held in 28 June 1848 on the policy to be adopted.
8. Colonial Office record of list of the five directors of Shell Overseas Exploration Company by December 1948.
9. A statement made on 6 August 1949, concerning the misunderstanding regarding the activities of Shell D'Arcy in the Eastern Provinces.
10. Letter of 25 June 1957, in reply to a representation from Standard Oil Company (New Jersey) indicating an interest to obtain a concession in the Western Region.

11. Letter of 4 July 1957, between London and Lagos Colonial Offices.
12. Oil Ordinance, Chapter 135.
13. Oil Exploration Licence No. 5, November 1955.
14. Oil Prospecting Licence No. 24, May 1957.

CHAPTER 3
The Civil War

The military coup of 15 January 1966[8] is an ignominious date in Nigerian history, as it signalled the beginning of military incursion into Nigerian politics. Ahmadu Bello (Premier of the Northern Region) was assassinated along with the Prime Minister, Tafawa Balewa. A counter-coup led by northern soldiers on 29 July 1966, resulted in the death of the then Igbo military head of state, General Johnson Aguiyi-Ironsi, and brought Colonel Yakubu Gowon to power.

Colonel Odumegwu Ojukwu, then governor of the Eastern Region, citing massive Igbo massacres in the North and electoral fraud, declared the state of Biafra on 30 May 1967. Several peace accords followed, but nothing was resolved.

The Nigeria-Biafra War officially started on 6 July 1967, and as the federal forces seemed to have the advantage, the British Cabinet decided, on 27 July 1967, that it would be in her majesty's government's best interest for Shell to make all payments of oil revenue to the federal government rather than Biafra. This betrayed the duplicity of the British government during the Nigeria-Biafra Civil War.

During the weeks that followed, it was reported in the Commonwealth office in Lagos, in a correspondence dated 23 June 1967, that Ojukwu was desperate for recognition of the state of Biafra and had told Mr. Parker of Lagos Commonwealth Office that Britain must lead the way to recognize Biafra. The way Ojukwu planned to achieve that was by putting pressure on the oil companies. Britain was faced with a bad situation, aggravated

---

8 This coup, also known as the "Coup of the Five Majors" was seen in the North as an Igbo coup against northern leadership.

by troubles in the Middle East and the likelihood of the oil flow being halted by either Ojukwu or Gowon, whichever of the oil companies offended.

The Nigerian government decided to effectively enforce a naval blockade, so much so, that any oil tanker attempting to run it would be intercepted and perhaps sunk. Shell-BP was badly tempted to pay, due to the existence of two new revenue decrees, one from Gowon's government and the other from Ojukwu's Biafra, demanding payment not later than 28 June 1967. Ojukwu's demand for a token payment went far beyond the provisions of his own legislation. Shell-BP was strongly urged not to make any payment in the time being because of the danger of offending one side or the other. The Commonwealth Office in Lagos strongly suggested that Shell-BP refused to make the token payment because it had no legal justification. A decision to make the payment would have amounted to a recognition of Biafra, a situation which would be resented and most certainly be counterproductive in Lagos.

The Lagos Commonwealth Office advised that if Shell-BP were determined to "pay the piper", it would be a mistake for the British government to associate itself with the company. Nevertheless, Shell-BP chose to make a token payment to Ojukwu, an act which displeased Gowon. In a flash from Lagos to the Commonwealth Office, London, it was reported that Shell-BP pleaded with Gowon to rescind the order stopping the oil flow, but Gowon declined at a meeting with Mr. Gray of Shell-BP on 5 July 1967. That meant production in the Mid-West and East would stop completely by night on 6 July 1967. By 5 July 1967, Safrap had stopped production.

Before and after Ojukwu pronounced the secession of the Eastern Region on 30 May 1967, enormous pressure had been mounted on the federal government to avoid an oil tanker blockade for the eastern routes. On 8 July 1967, the British minister of state for Commonwealth Affairs met with Major General Yakubu Gowon, at which meeting, a strong case was made by the minister for the blockade to be lifted to give way for oil shipments to continue. Gowon was adamant, insisting that it was not be in the best interest of Nigeria to do so.

On 13 July 1967, seven days after the war started, the Petroleum Control Decree 1967 was enacted by the federal military government. In section 9 (the power to revoke licences), very stringent provisions were made which sent a clear message to any offenders.

On 1 August 1967, the Biafran government announced the takeover of oil installations belonging to Shell-BP, which had been ordered to pay oil royalties, estimated to be £7 million.

The Nigerian Civil War disrupted the activities of the oil companies in the Eastern Region. *The Oil and Gas Journal* reported extensively on this on 20 January 1969. But the *Daily Telegraph* reported on 18 February 1969 that Nigerian oil was to come on stream again after the recovery of the territory occupied by Biafra since July 1967. Also, the *Petroleum Intelligence Weekly* reported on 22 February 1969 that a new mix of Nigerian crude oil may begin to flow to export markets by July 1 that year. However, the *Financial Times* on 29 July 1969 reported that a "Biafran air strike sets Shell Oil Station ablaze".

From the onset of the conflict, the British government had been concerned about the future of their interests in Nigeria. At a point, there were uncertainties in London on the position to take in the conflict. This was apparent in a document dated 24 August 1967, forwarded by the British High Commissioner in Nigeria to the Secretary of State for Commonwealth Affairs.

On 2 and 3 December 1968, the *Financial Times* and *Times of London* reported that Shell-BP had resumed production of oil in the war-damaged areas. Production was first limited to 200,000 barrels a day, because of damages to booster stations, pumps, and pipelines in the fields and the terminals. Before the war, Shell-BP was producing 500,000 barrels per day.

There were numerous exchanges in 1972 between various departments of the British government, calculating the consequences of Nigeria expropriating the assets of the British government, including BP. There were suggestions to reduce Britain's shareholding in BP and sell part of it to foreigners, so as to diversify the nationality of the ownership. While the battle on the participation negotiation between the OPEC nations and the consumer nations raged on, there was another participation battle between the oil companies and their host, which the oil companies in Nigeria had to face separately. That situation led to the Oil Consumer Cooperation versus Oil Producer Cooperation. A file note written on 6 August 1968, by one Shepherd to the British prime minister revealed that, in the early days of the Nigeria-Biafra war, Shell-BP was not sure where to camp, between the Federal Government of Nigeria and Biafra.

The relationship between the Nigerian and British government was strained, because of the former's attitude during the Rhodesian crisis. This coldness persisted to the days of the negotiation for participation in the oil sector. Negotiations dragged on, sometimes causing acrimony as could be seen in a letter dated 29 August 1972, from the British High Commissioner in Lagos to London on the negotiations between oil companies and the federal military government. Negotiations were difficult, but the Nigerian government maintained their position to the end and got what they wanted on the participation principle.

CHAPTER 4
When OPEC Came

The Organization of Petroleum Exporting Countries (OPEC) was formed by some developing nations as a platform for the safeguard and promotion of their national interests. The common problem which united the oil producing countries was the leverage of the multinational oil companies, which none of the oil-producing nations could stand up to then. By the creation of OPEC, members were equal to the might of the oil explorers. Nigeria did not join OPEC until 1971, when she had come of age in the oil producer and exporter community. At that time, the main goal of OPEC members was an enhanced involvement in the control and management of their petroleum resources. Such a goal was expected to lead to increased national revenue, employment generation, and political advancement in the international scene. OPEC's policies and goals served as eye-opener to the Nigerian government, whereupon the Nigerian National Oil Corporation (NNOC) was established in 1971, under the supervision of the Ministry of Mines and Power.

Following this development, some measures were taken to strengthen the petroleum industry. The Ministry of Petroleum and Energy was created in 1975, which absorbed the Department of Petroleum Resources and the Nigerian National Oil Corporation (NNOC). The petroleum sector was separated from the ministry in 1976, and yet another step was taken in 1977, which marked a major structural change in Nigeria's petroleum industry for good. This structural change led to the creation of the Nigerian National Petroleum Corporation (NNPC), by fusing the Ministry of Petroleum Resources and the Nigerian National Oil Corporation (NNOC). This marked a significant step in the development of the oil and gas sector.

Until 1960, government participation in the oil industry was limited to fiscal policies. Through the NNPC, the federal government became the dominant player in the downstream sector, by acquiring equity shares in all the international oil marketing companies. This was not without suspicion and reservations by the companies. The NNPC was vested with exclusive responsibility for upstream and downstream development, which covers exploration, exploiting, refining, and the marketing of crude oil. It supervises government investments in the industry through the National Petroleum Investment Management Services (NAPIMS). All NNPC upstream operations are managed under the Exploration and Production Directorate, which operates the following strategic business units (SBU) directly under the NNPC management:

1. National Petroleum Investment Management Services (NAPIMS)
2. Integrated Data Services Limited (IDSL)
3. Nigerian Petroleum Development Company (NPDC)
4. The Nigerian Gas Company Ltd. (NGC)
5. Nigeria Liquefied Natural Gas Ltd. (NLNG)
6. National Engineering and Technical Company Ltd. (NETCO)
7. Hydrocarbon Services Nigeria Ltd. (HYSON)
8. Warri Refinery and Petrochemical Co. Ltd. (WRPC)
9. Kaduna Refinery and Petrochemical Co. Ltd. (KRPC)
10. Port Harcourt Refining Co. Ltd. (PHRC)
11. Eleme Petrochemical Company Ltd.
12. Pipelines and Products Marketing Company

These strategic business units are collectively responsible for surveys, seismic data collation and interpretation, crude oil exploration, production, transportation, storage, and marketing. The downstream operation covers crude oil/gas conversion into refined petrochemical products, gas treatment, as well as the transportation and marketing of petroleum products. The downstream plants under the NNPC include three refineries, with a total installed capacity of 445,00 barrels per day, Port Harcourt (210,000 barrels per day), Warri (125,000 barrels per day), and

Kaduna (110,000 barrels per day). The three petrochemical plants in Warri, Kaduna, and Eleme, and some gas projects are also part of the downstream operations. There are some 5000 kilometres of pipelines, with twenty-one storage depots and nine liquefied petroleum gas (LPG) depots around the country.

On 25 November 1960, an agreement was reached in principle that Shell and British Petroleum Companies would jointly build a refinery in Port Harcourt. The refinery was to have the capacity to process 1,000,000 tonnes of crude oil per year. A company called Shell-BP Nigerian Petroleum Refining Company was incorporated to build and operate the refinery. It was noted earlier that the discovery of oil was made by Shell-BP, the sole concessionaire then. The first oil field came on stream in 1958, with a production of 5,100 barrels per day. After 1960, exploration rights were given to other foreign companies. By 1965, the EA field was discovered in shallow water south-east of Warri. By 1970, the year the Nigerian Civil War ended, there was a sharp rise in the price of oil, which earned Nigeria an instant fortune from oil production. Soon, production was reaching over 2,000,000 barrels per day and, then, the problem of capacity to manage the fortune became pronounced.

In 1974, NNPC's participation in the oil industry increased to 55 % and then 60 % in 1979. As the responsibilities of the NNPC grew, political pressure increased. The NNPC now became the economic pulse of the country, and the link between the government and the industry. Several structural changes were made to the NNPC which included, in 1987, the creation of the Petroleum Resources Management Division, to complement the Petroleum Inspectorate, to address any conflict inherent in the organization. Some of the reorganizations led to confusion or greater conflict between the political authority, symbolized by the ministry and the professionals. The NNPC carried out an internal reorganization in 1986, which resulted in the setting up of the strategic business units (SBUs) referred to earlier. The idea was to operate the SBUs as profit-making commercial units. In 1988, the Department of Petroleum Resources was removed from the

NNPC and taken back to the Ministry of Petroleum Resources, a decision which reawakened the problems instigated by the merger of the NNOC and the Ministry of Petroleum Resources to create the NNPC then. Before the issue was resolved, another reorganization took place, which converted the SBUs of the NNPC into quasi-independent subsidiary companies. This decentralization made the heads of the SBUs managing directors, while the chief executive officer of the NNPC became group managing director. The first reorganization referred to earlier occurred as a result of the report of the Irikefe Commission of Inquiry into the alleged loss of $2.8 billion from the account of the NNPC, which observed that the NNPC was too large to function efficiently. The fact that so much reorganization and restructure occurred within such a short time is ample testimony to the problems which the NNPC faced and their import for the oil and gas industry of the future.

Although the NNOC (the predecessor of the NNPC) was created as a result of a need to have an organization to oversee the commercial aspects of the oil industry, and in response to OPEC's intervention, which was an eye-opener for Nigeria, some factors worked against the realization of the objectives of the NNOC. There was no appropriate pricing regime, and because proper deregulation was absent, private investors had no incentive to invest in the industry, and in the absence of a subsidy regime, there was no profit motivation for investors.

The Western Region government which was the remaining shareholder in the Port Harcourt refinery had to surrender their shares in the end when they had to pay cash calls with no profit. As a result of the discouraging scenario, there was massive smuggling of products across the Nigerian border. Since then, the complex issue of deregulation has been with the oil industry because of weakness in the policy choice and implementation. Because of the insistence on the uniform pricing policy, the Kaduna refinery was followed by the construction of the Warri refinery, in the hope that their operations would stem the tide of smuggling to neighbouring countries.

The NNPC was also burdened with the policy of offering only one grade of petroleum product, which was unpopular with the consumers. The deregulation of the industry, which has been debated publicly for over two decades, remains the most contentious subject today. The federal government and industry operators want deregulation, but a majority of Nigerians are opposed to deregulation. In public eye, the NNPC epitomizes corporate evil and greed. However, the NNPC has no authority to deregulate because that policy power resides in the government, and this is one issue government is reluctant to address as any increase in the price of petrol is very unpopular with the electorate. A recent attempt to deregulate in January 2011 sparked a nationwide strike which paralysed the country for over one week.

CHAPTER 5

Regulatory Instruments and Practices

Legislation on petroleum has been in existence for some time before exploration was first undertaken. The first legislation was the Petroleum Ordinance of 1889, which was followed in 1907 by the Mineral Regulation (Oil) Ordinance. Both legislations provided the basic framework for the exploration and development of petroleum resources.

The 1907 law stipulated, inter alia, that only British subjects or companies controlled by British subjects were eligible to carry out oil exploration in Nigeria. This was to protect the sovereign interests of Great Britain. Regardless of the stipulation on oil exploration eligibility, the Nigerian Bitumen Company (owned by German nationals) was the first to ever undertake exploration, in 1908, in what is now part of present-day Ondo State. No one can claim to know the details of the Nigerian Bitumen Company, but it was curious that the company was given right to explore for bitumen at all. It was likely that the company had any British interest.

The next concession was given to Shell-D'Arcy (later known as Shell-BP Petroleum Development Company) in 1938, covering, land mass of about 375,000 square miles on the mainland of Nigeria. It dominated exploration and was able to explore choice acreage until 1962, when its original 375,000 square miles holding was reduced considerably. In 1959, the concessionary rights were reviewed to extend rights to other companies such as Mobil, Gulf (now Chevron), Agip, Safrap (Elf), Texaco, and Amoseas (Texaco/Chevron). Owing to the former monopolistic concessionary position, Shell remains the largest producer of oil in Nigeria, holding about 80 % of all concessions. In 1969, the existing petroleum legislation was repealed by the Petroleum Act 1969 (Decree No. 51). The Act and its accompanying Petroleum (Drilling and Publication) Regulations provided the foundation of the legal framework for the regulation of the Nigerian oil industry.

Shortly after this, the Nigerian National Oil Corporation (NNOC) was established and, by July 1971, Nigeria joined OPEC (Organization of Petroleum Exporting Countries). The 1969 Petroleum Decree marked Nigeria's first step in establishing ownership and control of all petroleum on any land to which the Act applied. This applied to all lands in Nigeria, under the territorial waters of Nigeria and part of the continental shelf. This Act repealed the Mineral Oil Act (whole), Minerals Act (some words), Petroleum Act (whole), Petroleum Fuel Act (whole), and Petroleum Control Decree 1967 (section 7).

Since the 1969 Act changed the nature of the oil industry completely, negotiations started in earnest between the oil companies and the federal government; which led to the first participation agreement with Elfin 1971, in which the government acquired 35 % interest in the Elf concessions. Similarly, government acquired 35 % interest in Shell-BP, Mobil, and Gulf concessions, respectively, in 1973. The interests held by the Nigerian government have increased over time to the level of 65 %, except for Shell, in which government interest increased to 80 %, in consequence of the nationalization of BP in 1979. Since then, changes in policy have reduced in stages the level of interest in BP to 55 % to accommodate other liquefied gas partners.

In 1972, the Nigerian National Oil Corporation, the predecessor to the Nigerian National Petroleum Corporation, was assigned all areas in the country not covered by existing licences or leases, and also any concessionary areas held by other oil companies, which might be surrendered from time to time. It was announced in 1973 that no further concessions would be granted to any company, organization, or individuals, but the NNOC could select other companies as contractors or partners in executing its concessions. Although these policy measures were not drawn up into any legislation, they were regulatory instruments which had great impact on the present legal framework.

In July 1977, the Nigerian National Petroleum Corporation (NNPC) was established, a step which ended the existence of the Nigerian National Oil Corporation (NNOC). Oil prices fell sharply with the glut of the 1980s. In response, the federal government entered into the first memorandum of understanding (MoII) with the oil companies in 1986. Another MoU was signed in 1991, while the third was signed in August 2000. All the memoranda of understanding guaranteed a profit margin to the oil companies.

Since oil and gas emerged in the Nigerian economy, several laws have been brought to bear on the direction of the industry, such as the Oil and Pipelines Act of 1956, Petroleum Profits Tax Act of 1959, and various Associated Gas Reinjection Acts. The Petroleum Act of 1969[9] and the Petroleum (Drilling and Production) Regulations[10] formed the backbone of the regulatory instruments of the oil industry. The Act stated that only Nigerians, or companies incorporated in Nigeria, may be granted the following rights:

a. An exploration licence to explore for petroleum
b. An oil mining lease to search for, win, work, carry away, and dispose of petroleum.

All the rights stipulated size of territory. The Petroleum (Drilling and Production) Regulations were made in pursuance of the powers vested in the ministry by Article 9 of the Petroleum Act. They addressed exhaustively various matters relating to the form and method of application for prospecting licences and leases, and the rights and powers of licensees and lease holders. The regulations have comprehensive provisions covering all imaginable aspects of petroleum drilling, including technical and administrative matters. Since their inception, the Act and Regulations have remained, with only some amendments such as the

---

9 Petroleum Act 1969: Reg. 2 (1).
10 Petroleum (Drilling and Production Regulation), 1969.

Marginal Fields Decree of 1996 and the Deep Offshore and Inland Basin Production Sharing Decree of 1999. Several other policy steps have been taken over the years, which seek to regulate the oil and gas industry to the best interests of Nigeria and the oil companies.

A casual look at the amount of legal instruments created since the emergence of oil in Nigeria easily suggests that capacity was built for the efficient management of the oil and gas industry. However, experience has shown beyond doubt that regulatory capacity through legal instruments is of little value unless the human capacity is available in adequate measure to oversee the industry. This was clearly not the case as can be seen when examining the factors which have interfered with the achievement of the desired results by the NNPC and affiliates. Some of the other regulatory instruments include the following:

- Petroleum Ordinance of 1889
- Mineral Regulation (Oil) Ordinance of 1907
- Order No. 19 of the 1909 Laws of Southern Nigeria
- Mineral Oils Ordinance of 1914 (Cap. 120 of the Laws of the Federation of 1958 edition)
- Mineral Oils Act (Amendment) of 1950
- Mineral Oils Act (Amendment) of 1959
- Petroleum Profits Tax of 1959
- Petroleum Profits Tax (Amendment) Decree of 1967
- Oil Terminal Dues Act of 1969 (retroactive from 1965)
- Production Sharing Contract, 1973.

CHAPTER 6

Leases and Licences

From the beginning of 1962, Shell-BP was to surrender about half of its holdings for which it held prospecting licences. A conference was held between the Nigerian government and the oil companies, at which an agreement was reached in the form of the licences to be issued with the exception of two points. The Nigerian government wanted the existing method of calculating the price of oil on which royalty payments were based to continue, while some oil companies wanted a different method. The existing method was that the price on which royalties were calculated was the price received in Europe by Shell-BP less transport costs from the field storage tank to the European refineries. Some companies argued that the price be based on world prices. Although the disagreement appeared at one stage to be a major one, the differences were narrowed down.

The Ministry of Mines and Power also wanted the companies' obligations to include the establishment of refineries in Nigeria in a way that the Nigerian government could instruct the refining companies to sell the refined products to particular countries. The nil companies refused to accept the proposal. The renewed prospecting licences and mining leases resulting from that conference held in 1961 affected Shell-BP only on the Continental Shelf. Shell-BP was to continue to operate under their old licences, and leases, which were based on the Colonial Office standard model in the land areas. The other companies were to be affected, in their operations both on the Continental Shelf and on any land. The other companies were given an opportunity to explore the land surrendered by Shell-BP when they came on the market.

By 31 May 1961, Shell-BP, Gulf, Mobil, Tennessee Gas and a Joint Texaco and Stancal had applied for off-shore concessions. The terms of the draft licences were reported by the companies to contain four unacceptable clauses. One of these clauses provided that in the event of any discrimination against Nigeria or Nigerian nationals by the directors of a company, the concession would be revoked without any right of appeal. Shell-BP objected to this clause on the grounds that the company could be penalized for events entirely outside its control. Shell-BP was incorporated in Nigeria, but if Britain or Holland did anything to upset Nigeria, Shell-BP's licence might be revoked or modified. Gulf Oil was particularly concerned about the clause in view of the troubles with Freedom Riders in Alabama, USA.

The revised oil licences and leases on which agreements had been reached were signed on 30 September 1961. Licences were granted to Gulf Oil, not only for ten blocks on the Continental Shelf, but also for a substantial land area near Port Harcourt The land area was part of the portion already explored by Shell-BP and given up by them for a premium of about £600,000.

The licences signed on 30 September 1961, did not come into effect until the premium had been paid, and they were not to be paid until certain negotiations with the Ministry of Finance were completed by the oil companies. The oil companies wanted a written understanding that even if the Petroleum Profit Tax Ordinance of 1959 that established the 50/50 principle which was then repealed, its terms would nevertheless continue to govern the taxation of profits from the production in the areas covered by the licences that were just issued to the companies. Shell-BP already had such an understanding for their onshore concessions.

By February 1970, half of Nigeria's rich seabed oil concessions were offered for reallocation as new concessions. Oil companies were invited on 5 February to apply for new concessions. The new licences were to have a five-year term and could be converted into mining leases. Shell-BP and Gulf Oil were exporting about 800,000 barrels per day; while Mobil, with offshore concessions in the eastern Calabar area, was expected to start producing about 50,000 barrels a day by March 1970. On 5 February 1970, Mobil announced that it had reached an agreement with the south-eastern state government in Calabar, for the construction of an oil terminal in the state.

The terms under which the new offshore licences were granted were covered by a new oil legislation published in November 1969. The terms were stricter than those covering concessions granted before 1962, when Nigeria was less experienced in oil matters. All applicants were to be incorporated in Nigeria, and fees of between £50,000 and £100,000 were payable for each of the 27 oil blocks offered. A new element was that the Nigerian government reserved the right 'by itself or through any of its designated agencies..., to participate up to an agreed percentage in each licence' and, after five years, in the resulting leases. It was clear that the government intended to drive a fairly hard bargain, not only through participation, but in other ways. Government, for instance, insisted that all new concessionaires must contribute towards courses in petroleum technology, and should state clearly what other 'advantageous benefits' they intended to offer government in addition to those imposed statutorily.

The concessions then being offered were relinquished under the terms of the agreement signed in 1968 by Shell-BP, Texaco, Gulf, Mobil and American Overseas Petroleum.

In New York, Global Energy Company (25 % owned by New York and Honduras Rosario Mining) announced that it had been given oil concessions in Nigeria to the tune of some 70,609 square miles.

On 30 June 1970, R.A.B. Dikko, Nigeria's commissioner for mines and power, announced some new concessions given to other oil companies (which included some 2,500 square miles of coastal waters). The companies included one American concern, one West German, one Japanese and two Nigerian. All the winners were getting their first stakes in Nigeria. Germany's Deminex Group was awarded blocks 74, 76, 80 and 83; Japanese Petroleum (formed by Mitsui, Tiejin and Teikoka Oil) got blocks 72, 73, 86 and 92, while Occidental Petroleum got blocks 85, 87, 88 and 90. A Nigerian company, Henry Stephens, was reported to have got block 89. Monsanto Chemicals was given two or four blocks, while one or two went to Leventis.

No awards were given to the existing producers or concession holders, although some of them submitted applications, including Mobil, Texaco and Safrap. Bidders who missed out were Cities Service, Royal Resources, Union Oil, Standard of Indiana's Amoco, Syracuse Oil (a Canadian firm) and Delta Oil.

No concessions were made on some choice blocks, which were set aside in reserve for future development. Safrap and all the American majors, with the exception of Esso, did not receive concessions. Of course, Safrap could not have been expected to be awarded a concession at that time, as they had not even been permitted to resume production from their field at Obaji. The government wisely reserved about half of the acreage, made up of twelve blocks, mainly onshore, and concentrated on the two most promising areas. A curious feature of the allocation is that some companies received acreage for which they did not apply.

The general effect of the new concessions was that established companies, notably Shell-BP, were faced with new competitors who might weaken their monopolistic front. This chapter is strictly an historical account of the interplay between government and oil companies, regarding the administration of concessions. Whether a concession is for oil exploration, oil prospecting or oil mining, the oil companies require the approval of the federal government to commence exploration, prospecting or production.

The upstream licences of several oil companies expired in December 2008, but the Nigerian government informed them of its intention to renew the leases with new terms. ExxonMobil succeeded in renewing its licence under a 20-year renewable extension for three of its shallow-water licences – OMLs 67, 68 and 70, which it has operated since 1968 as a joint venture with the Nigerian National Petroleum Corporation (NNPC).

In November 2008, five of Shell's licences were up for renewal: OMLs 71, 72, 74, 77 and 79. Shell had gone to court, in 2008, to challenge the decision to renew contracts on new terms, but had to retract the lawsuit it had lodged in November 2008 in order to be considered.[11] Because of its pioneering role in the Nigerian oil industry, Shell has enjoyed a great advantage with respect to concession sites. Thus, the company's early monopoly with regard to site choice and licence award gives it a position of dominance even today.

Before 1969, the oil companies required government approval before the commencement of exploration, development or production, as provided in Section 3 of the Mineral Oil Ordinance of 1914. Prior to 1959, the minister of mines and power negotiated the concessionary agreements with each interested oil company. Since 1959, the acquisition of oil rights became standardized.

The standardization distinguished between exploration, prospecting and mining rights.[12] The nature of an oil exploration licence (OEL) was that the oil company had the right to conduct geophysical and geographical exploration for oil over land and water, excluding land already granted to operators. An OEL was granted for one-year duration, subject to renewal for another year. It could be upgraded to a prospecting licence in an area with good prospects for oil. An OEL could be granted to more than one company in the same concession area, for up to 10,000 square miles.

As for an oil prospecting licence (OPL), this is in respect of the mainland including a 3-mile coastal limit and the Continental Shelf area. An OPL is valid for three years, renewable for another two years, while the Continental Shelf area licence is valid for four years, renewable for three years. A prospecting licence guarantees the company's exclusive right to carry out geological and geophysical investigations in its concession areas to drill, export and refine petroleum. The holder of the OPL was strictly obliged to commence geophysical investigation within six months and drill

---

11 Nigeria Oil and Gas Report Quarter 2, 2011. Business Monitor International Ltd., 2011.
12 Lawrence Atsegbua, The development and acquisition of oil licences and leases in Nigeria, OPEC Review, 1999; 23 (1): 55–77.

not less than 12,000 feet of wells on the mainland within three years, and four years in respect of the Continental Shelf. There were also several financial obligations attached to the grant. At the expiration of an OPL, it must be returned to the government or converted into a mining lease. In the case of oil mining leases (OML), they were granted for 30 years on land, 40 years on the Continental Shelf, with a right to renew for 40 years. The lessee has an exclusive right to take every measure necessary to exploit and to develop a project in its concession area. In addition to some other obligations, the lessee also had some financial obligations. The OEL, OPL and OML granted under the Mineral Oils Ordinance of 1914 were the concessionary rights for oil companies before equity participation and contractual joint venture systems came into being in 1969 and 1973.[13]

---

13 Lawrence Atsegbua, Nigerian Petroleum Law, Benin, New Era Publishers, 1993.

CHAPTER 7
Participation Agreements

The first hint of intention of the Nigerian government to participate directly in the oil industry appeared in a letter to the Colonial Office on 17 August 1949. Shell Overseas Exploration Company wrote on behalf of their partner, D'Arcy Exploration Company, in a reaction to the proposal by the Nigerian colonial government to have the right to nominate a representative to the board of the company and have shareholding participation. The message in the letter was that if granting shareholding participation was important politically, it is evident that it will cease to have political influence once it had been granted. Shell and D'Arcy felt that there could be the possibility of the government member of the board coming under political pressure to promote short-term policies, which would be detrimental to the normal and constructive development of the industry. With regard to the question 'in the absence of a government shareholding, whether it would be possible for Shell-D'Arcy to carry on their operations', they stressed that they were prepared to take the risk, since they felt that it would be possible to obtain recognition of the obvious benefits of the enterprise to the Nigerian economy. It was firmly stated by the companies that they were not prepared to spend several million pounds in a venture which might be jeopardized through the introduction of considerations of a non-commercial nature.

In the Second National Development Plan (1970–1974), which was published in November 1970, the federal military government made clear their desire to participate in all phases of the oil industry exploration and mining, refining, and distribution and marketing. The oil industry was included in the list of four, in which the government intended to have equity participation of at least 55 %. The vehicle for the participation was the Nigerian National Oil Corporation (NNOC), which was established in April 1971.

The federal government already had a 60 % control in the oil refinery at Port Harcourt and was determined to have complete ownership of a second refinery. Apart from 51 % participation options in the new offshore concessions at that time, the only move so far made into the crude oil-producing companies had been through the NNOC into the French Safrap and the Italian Agip/Phillips operations. In the case of Safrap, participation was required by the federal military government in exchange for permitting the company to resume operations after the civil war, because of French support for Biafra. The arrangement with Safrap provided for an immediate 35 % interest, which was to increase to 50 %, when production reached 250,000 barrels per day at a level of 400,000 barrels per day. In the case of Agip/Phillips, the NNOC took 33.3 % interest. This derived from the option provided in respect of future government participation in the original licensing agreement with Agip, who were later joined by Phillips as equal partners.

The Nigerian government later opened negotiations foil participation with the other four oil producers. The first meeting was held with Shell-BP, while meetings with Gulf and Mobil were to take place two weeks later. It was understood that the government's bid was so high as to make it impossible for companies to entertain it as a basis for negotiation. Negotiations were suspended. When negotiations resumed, the positions of both parties were poles apart. One John Wilson of the Foreign Office informed one of his colleagues, as seen in a file note on Nigerian oil, that

"… Nigerians had been unable to find a suitable staff for their national oil company though they had sourced the world for such staff. This only showed how impossible it was for them to take over, in practice, a share of managing the oil enterprise in Nigeria at present."

This remark clearly shows the problems which the NNOC faced from its inception, as a vehicle to actualize the ambition of the Nigerian government concerning the oil industry. Early in 1973, the Nigerian government stated that they had acquired 35 % of all the assets of Shell-BP with effect from 1 April of that year. By 1982, the federal government would possess 51 % of the entire operations of the oil company.

CHAPTER 8

Joint Venture Arrangements

Activities in the upstream sector include oil and gas exploration, prospecting, production, as well as crude oil storage and its evacuation through the pipelines to vessels for shipment. The operating arrangements in this sector are joint ventures (JV) or production sharing agreement (PSA). In the joint venture arrangement, oil-producing companies sign into agreement with the NNPC for the collaborative development of jointly held exploration licences and facilities. Each partner in the venture contributes to the costs, and shares the profits or losses of the operation according to proportionate equity interests in the ventures. One of the partners is designated the operator and is responsible for the running of the venture, but all budgets, work programmes and contracts awarded must be agreed to by all partners.

A regular feature of the upstream sector is the failure of the NNPC to meet its own cash call obligations whenever it has to pay. This feature often causes needless cutbacks in the exploration and production activities planned by the operators. The production sharing contract (PSC) came as a result of the difficulties faced by the NNPC to promptly fund joint venture operations and the need to increase oil reserves.

In the system, NNPC engaged competent contractors to carry out operations on NNPC's solely owned acreages. The contractor undertakes the initial exploration risks and recovers its costs if oil is found in commercial quantity. If oil is not found, the contractor receives nothing. Under the PSC, the contractor has full right to cost oil (oil to recoup production cost) and equity oil (oil to cover return on investment). The contractor can also dispose of the tax oil (oil to defray tax and royalty obligations) on behalf of NNPC. The balance of the oil is then shared between the contractor and NNPC (profit oil).

Nearly all deep-water explorations are conducted under this kind of contract. The oil companies involved so far are Shell, Mobil, Chevron, Agip, Elf, BP, Statoil, Esso/Dupont, Conoco and some indigenous companies.[14] Each joint venture operates under a joint operating agreement (JOA) with the NNPC, and memorandum of understanding (MoU) with the Nigerian government. The JOA defines relationships regarding:
1. Operator and obligations
2. Work programme plans and expenditure
3. Right of assignment by parties to the joint ventures
4. Off-take, scheduling and lifting procedures
5. Accounting procedure
6. Project contract procedures
7. Communication procedures

As mentioned in the overview of joint venture arrangements, all petroleum production and exploration are undertaken under JV between international oil companies and the Federal Government of Nigeria, with the NNPC as the agent. These JV account for approximately 95 % of all crude oil output, while indigenous independent companies operating in the marginal fields account for 5 %. Six companies now operate in Nigeria, which include Royal Dutch Shell (British/Dutch), Chevron (American), ExxonMobil (American), Agip (Italian), Total (French) and Texaco (merged with Chevron).

A joint venture operated by Shell accounts for 50 % of Nigeria's total oil production from more than 80 oil fields. This joint venture includes NNPC (55 %), Shell (30 %), TotalFinElf (10 %) and Agip (5 %). It operates largely onshore or in the mangrove swamp in the Niger Delta. The company has over one hundred oil-producing fields, and a network of over 6,000 km of pipeline, flowing through some ninety flow stations.

Shell owns concessions in Shell Petroleum Development Company (SPDC), Shell Nigeria Exploration and Production Compa-

---

14 Wikipedia, Petroleum in Nigeria, 2009.

ny (SNEPCO), Shell Nigeria (SNG), Shell Nigeria Oil Products (SNOP) and is holding of major stake in the Nigeria Liquefied Natural Gas (NLNG).

Chevron Nigeria Ltd (NCL), a joint venture between the NNPC (60 %) and Chevron (40 %), was in the past, the second largest oil producer, located in the Warri region west of the Niger River and offshore in shallow water.

Mobil Producing Nigeria Unlimited (MPNU) is a joint venture lift between the NNPC (60 %) and Exxon Mobil (40 %), operating in shallow water off Akwa Ibom State, in the south-eastern delta, making it the second largest producer. Mobil also holds a 50 % interest in a PSC for a deep-water block further offshore.

Nigerian Agip Oil Company Limited (NADC) is a joint venture operated by and owned by the NNPC (60 %), Agip (20 %) and ConocoPhillips (20 %). The company produces from mostly small onshore fields. Total Petroleum Nigeria Limited (TPNL) is a joint venture between NNPC (60 %) and Elf (now Total) (40 %) producing both on and offshore. The NNPC Texaco-Chevron Joint Venture is operated by Texaco, and owned by NNPC (60 %), Texaco (20 %) and Chevron (20 %) from offshore fields.

CHAPTER 9

Exploration and Production Contracts

Of the various contract options available to suit the nature of oil exploration worldwide, the NNPC chose four kinds of legal relationships for crude oil production to regulate Nigeria's oil and gas industry:
a. The concession contract
b. The joint venture contract
c. The production sharing contract, and
d. The service contract

When the government acquired participation interests in the concessions held by the oil companies, the joint venture contract replaced the concession contract (CC), which had dominated the relationship between the Nigerian government and oil companies. Under the arrangement, the relationship became regulated by the participation agreement and the operating agreement. The joint venture agreement is again regulated by another agreement called the memorandum of understanding (MoU). The production sharing contract (PSC) was adopted by the Nigerian government a policy shift from outright concessions towards emphasis on the contractual status of oil-producing companies. As a result, the government signed the first PSC with Ashland Oil Company in June 1973, for a period of 20 years.[15] That contract evoked some disquiet in the public eye, because it was believed that the terms of the contract were poorly worded to the advantage of the oil contractor. According to the agreement, when oil had been found in commercial value,

---

15 David N. Smith, Mineral agreements in developing countries: Structure and substance, American Journal of International Law, 1988; 69 (560): 1501–2000.

the costs were recoverable at a maximum of 50 % per annum of the total crude oil produced by the oil company. In Ashland's case, 55 % of the balance was allocated to the company as oil tax, and the price received was applied towards payment of petroleum profit tax (PPT). The balance of the amount payable as tax was borne by the government and Ashland in proportion to their participation interest shares. The remaining crude oil, minus 25 % of total production, was shared between both parties. When production was less than 50,000 barrels per day, the sharing was 65/35 in favour of Ashland and 79/30 when production was more.

In the opinion of industry experts and the Nigerian public, production sharing contracts (PSC) did not benefit Nigeria at all. The situation called for a review of the existing PSCs. The stage was set for completely new terms. In 1992 and 1993, the Nigerian National Petroleum Corporation (NNPC) negotiated contract terms with Ashland Exploration, Mobil Producing, Elf, Agip, BP Statoil/BP, Esso and Shell Nigeria Exploration and Production Company (SNEPCO). All the revised contracts covered periods of 30 years exploration and 20 years production, with strict provisions for relinquishment of part of the contract areas. The terms were substantially of the same spirit, but with some modifications. They generally provided for tax oil in negotiated quantities to be allocated to the NNPC for the payment of PPT. This rate was later given a legal seal in Section 3 (1) of Deep Offshore and Inland Basin Production Sharing Contracts Decree of 1999, which amended the PPT Act. Royalty oil is also allocated to NNPC for the payment of royalty and concession rentals on behalf of the contractor and the NNPC. Each contract is ring-fenced so that costs on one contract area cannot be deducted from the revenue accruing from another contract area. Cost oil (CO) is also allocated to the contractor for the recovery of operating and capital costs (OCC). Operating costs are recovered in the year of expenditure, while capital costs are recoverable in equal instalments over a five-year duration, or over the balance of the life of the contract, whichever is less.

The fragmentation of production varies from one PSC to mother. For instance, in the contract between NNPC and SNEPCO in April 1993, the following percentages were obtained:

Accumulative production profit MMB	Profit oil (%) NNPC	Profit oil (%)
0–350	20	80
351–750	35	65
751–1000	45	55
1001–1500	50	50
1501–2000	60	40

These splits are similar to the contract with Esso. The profit sharing ratio (PSR) in the NNPC/Statoil contract favours Statoil at lower production levels, up to one million barrels cumulative production. To curb excessive expenditure by the contractor, limits are stipulated beyond which the contractor must seek the approval of the NNPC. Thus, in the contract with Statoil, the approval of the NNPC must be obtained for purchases in excess of $100,000. The allocation of crude oil proceeds is in a priority order of royalty oil cost oil, tax oil and profit oil, which means that profit oil can only apply when the proceeds are available. Allocations are made on a monthly basis according to the previously agreed ratios.

CHAPTER 10
The Trouble with NNPC

Within a period of three years, during the new democratic dispensation, the Nigerian National Petroleum Corporation (NNPC) was taken through the leadership of five group managing directors (GMD), a pattern which undermined the policy locus and the development of Nigeria's oil and gas industry. One GMD was replaced barely one month after he was appointed. These rapid, perhaps, ill-conceived changes, were unmindful of the negative image which the instability sends to the international oil companies.

Funso Kupolokun was replaced by Abubakar Lawal Yar'Adua, who was replaced by Mohammed Sanusi Barkindo, after what was described as a grinding tenure of sixteen months, noted for uninspiring leadership. Sanusi Barkindo's appointment brought hope to the industry, because of his international background and disposition, but his tenure was marked by constant disagreements with the National Assembly, and his uncompromising view on the Petroleum Industry Bill (in which the oil companies showed considerable interest). Barkindo's leadership provided a good insight concerning the transformation of the NNPC, from a stereotyped national oil company to a properly run international oil company.

Surprisingly, Barkindo was replaced in April 2010 by Shehu Ladan who had been disengaged from the NNPC in April 2009.

That appointment came as a reminder to the troubles with the way the NNPC was taken from one port to another by various governments. By May 2010, about one month into Shehu Ladan's tenure, his appointment was terminated and Austen Oniwon was appointed as the group managing director, from his post as group executive director of refining and petrochemicals. Government announced that the accounts of the NNPC would be scrutinized, which suggested that financial misconducts may have been noticed in the affairs of the NNPC. No one is in doubt that the poor performance of the NNPC should be blamed largely on the government's inability to ensure the freedom of the NNPC from heavy political influence.

Between 2007 and 2010, some major policy decisions have had to be delayed or changed because of the unstable atmosphere in government and in the NNPC. Some projects such as Chevron's Nsiko, Shell's Bonga SW/NW, Aparo, Olokola LNG and Brass LNG trains 7 and 8 are among the projects these delays affected.

Shell announced that the Forcados Yokri and Bonga Northwest projects, which were due to come onstream in 2010 or 2011, will be delayed, with the Bonga Northwest being tendered again. This has serious financial implications. With Nigeria's rating as one of the most corrupt and poorly governed countries in Africa south of the Sahara, even the best chief executive officers in the world cannot raise NNPC's performance bar.

It has been estimated that about 300,000 barrels of crude oil are stolen every day. Under military rule, it was presumed that the top officers were behind the theft commonly known as bunkering. More than one decade after military rule, the practice continues and is even more pronounced. In 2003, Shell alone lost about 200,000 barrels of oil per day to theft. Who are the thieves? The government does not know, and even NNPC, the curator of Nigeria's oil resources and the regulator, does not know as well.

When oil was struck in 1956, Nigeria was unprepared for the challenges which the development brought. Oil started to flow two years after, but the only semblance of capacity was the existence of the Department of Petroleum Resources. From the pioneer Department of Petroleum Resources to the ministry, then to the creation of the Nigerian National Oil Corporation (NNOC) and, ultimately, the establishment of the Nigerian National Petroleum Corporation, the capacity-building efforts were based on the stereotyped civil service culture. That foundation became increasingly unable to bear the burden of performance being thrust on the NNPC, in an industry that is characterized by the dictates of the international market. That factor led to the need for repeated restructuring, reorganization and management changes, some of which had little effect.

Heavy losses threaten the NNPC, as liabilities totalling about $2.5 billion are pushing the Nigerian oil giant into bankruptcy. This has become public knowledge, and the government has owned up in the fact that if the crisis is not arrested, the NNPC will cease to exist. This is the main objective of the Petroleum Industry Bill (PIB), Technically, the NNPC is insolvent. In 2009, it lost N25 billion in revenue, and claimed it spent about N800 billion on fuel importation. Between 2000 and 2009, about N175 billion was spent to repair vandalized pipelines. In 2009 alone, about 132 million litres of petroleum products were lost to theft and diversion. In addition, the inefficiency is deepened by a multiplicity of roles, which puts a dead weight on the company.

By September 2011, oil watchers had revealed a lot on the large-scale corruption that ravages both the nation and its institutions. It was revealed that highly-placed Nigerians, senior military officers, Lebanese, Iranian, British and American businessmen are involved in oil theft. Some experts put the annual loss at about 91 million barrels of crude oil.

One of the sources gave details of how the illegal bunkering is operated, a revelation that shows the decay in the Nigerian oil and gas industry. High-ranking military officers are reported to give protection to the barges of operators, which include operators of oil tankers and tanker terminals, employees of major international oil companies and local contractors. Oil bunkering is one of the world's biggest black markets, but authorities turn a blind eye when highly-placed figures are involved in this racket. It is thus the greatest threat to the oil industry.

The other aspect of the problem is the anger and violence visited on oil installations by militant gangs, who claim to be fighting for the rights of the Niger Delta people, whose region has been devastated by environmental degradation, occasioned by pollution. For instance, the leaders of the gangs have openly admitted that the Niger Delta is the owner of all the oil and they have the right to do whatever they want with their oil. The war against the militants has never been curtailed despite the heavy military presence. It was not until an amnesty was offered that the militants agreed to lay down their arms, but at a great cost.

Oil bunkering still thrives, but in a more sophisticated pattern. The smugglers have proved elusive and desperate. After filling their barges with oil, armed smugglers move the barges down the river to load up the larger tankers in open waters and head for faraway buyers.

In one interesting episode, the Nigerian Navy intercepted a large tanker loader with crude valued $162,000. According to investigation, the owner of the tanker was a retired army officer. The owner's bank account and assets were frozen, but the smuggler disappeared before he was charged to court. Yet another case arose in which the 12,000-tonne *Africa Pride*, a ship, bearing some 80,000 barrels of crude oil was intercepted. The ship was seized and tied up at the Lagos wharf, and the crewmen were jailed.

The tanker was under the watch of the Nigerian Navy, but it disappeared under laughable circumstances. Three senior officers of the Navy were court-martialled, while two of them were dismissed with ignominy. These episodes eloquently illustrate the frustration of those who insist that the Nigerian oil industry should be saved from the evil scourge of corruption.

In a damning, but honest verdict in 2007, *The Economist*[16] described the NNPC as a source of corruption and national-shame, and wondered whether reform was possible. Nobody in government seems to have the solution to bunkering, while corruption has become a real threat to the stability of the nation.

---

16 Nigeria: Reforming the Oil Industry, The Economist, 2007: 384 (8545): 51.

CHAPTER 11
Oil Refining

In the mining leases granted to Shell-BP Petroleum Development Company, it was specified that as soon as the output of crude oil from the areas leased to them amounted, in the aggregate, to 500,000 tonnes per annum, the oil company shall consider, with the minister of mines and power, the economic feasibility of the establishment of a refinery capable of supplying the local requirements of motor gasoline and fuel oil. By 1960, it was reported that production had reached about 850,000 tonnes per annum. Shell-BP had sent an exploratory team to Nigeria in 1959, to conduct a preliminary reconnaissance. Another team visited Nigeria to negotiate the terms for the establishment of a refinery. The refinery was to be sited near Port Harcourt, and it was hoped that the refinery would go into operation in 1964. In a White Paper published in November 1960,[17] it was clearly stated that it was agreed between Shell-BP and the federal government that at a suitable time after the commencement of operations, both parties would give earnest consideration to the possibility of the federal government taking up the financial interest in the refineries. The governor-general's speech indicated that:

"... now that agreement has been reached between my government and the Shell-BP Refinery Company, plans will go forward for the erection of a refinery near Port Harcourt, with financial participation by my government and such of the regional governments as so desire."[18]

---

[17] Federation of Nigeria. Establishment of Oil Refinery in Nigeria. Session Paper No. 5, Federal Government Press, Lagos, 1960.

[18] File notes between J.S. Sadler and J.A. Davidson of Commonwealth Relations Office, London in 1960 on the proposal to establish oil refinery in Nigeria.

In the opinion of Shell-BP, who negotiated all the way for the establishment of the refinery, the statement represented a drastic change in the attitude of the federal government. This was as a result of pressure from the Eastern Region Government, which would be host to the Port Harcourt Refinery. There were indications that officials of the Federal Ministry of Finance were of the view that government participation in the oil refinery from the outset would be wrong for two major reasons:

1. The federal government could be accused of bad faith if it insisted on taking a share of the equity after their statement in the White Paper mentioned earlier.
2. There were many claims on the resources of the federal government, and it would be an unprofitable use of the limited resources to spend them on a project which foreign investors were quite willing to pay for.

In spite of the validity and respectability of reservations expressed by the civil servants, the advice was rejected. Understandably, for good reasons, Shell-BP was reluctant to agree to the request by the Nigerian government. In the correspondence between the United Kingdom Trade Commissioner in Lagos and the Commonwealth Relations Office in London in March 1961, it was clear that there was disquiet over the decision to invest government funds in the project. It was viewed by the Foreign Office that if the Nigerian government put a substantial sum of money into the refinery, as they were intending to, it would be a clear evidence of the tendency of the Nigerian ministers failing to understand that their financial resources were limited and that if the government spent money on one project, which it should not do, there would be that much loss for some other important projects. This was logical thinking.

Another record of correspondence in the Commonwealth Relation's Office indicates that the view that the Nigerian government should take a 51 % share in the capital of the proposed oil refinery was advanced by the NCNC ministers, as against the somewhat half-hearted doubtful stance taken by the Prime Minister, Tafawa Balewa, and the minister of Mines and Power. The NCNC was the only political party in the coalition government of the Balewa administration. The prime minister seemed to have been particularly concerned about how the funds could be raised by the government. The government of the Eastern Region had already indicated that it would take up £1 million of the equity. Both the Northern and Western Region governments had also indicated that they would take part of the equity.

Although the financing of the shares by the governments was serious problem, the more dangerous consequence of the decision seemed to be its possible effect on other private investors contemplating investment in Nigeria. It seemed quite plausible to guess that such investors' confidence in the good faith of the Nigerian government would be severely shaken. In the meantime, Shell-BP had made it clear to the federal authorities in Lagos that they would not be prepared to participate in the building of a refinery if they would have only a minority share in the company. Shell-BP's reasons were obvious and reasonable, namely that the Nigerian directors of the refinery would at best distract the management and, at worst, make their job quite difficult through needless interference and costly bureaucracy.

After a fairly long period of suspended negotiations, discussions were resumed in August 1961, on the initiative of the federal government. Shell-BP was asked to consider if they would be prepared to hold 30 % and the federal government held 40 %, while 30 % was divided among the other oil companies.

A second refinery was already being contemplated in 1970, and a decision in principle had been made to locate it in the Lagos area. BP's competitors in the construction of the Lagos project were a team headed by Mobil, which included Texaco, Agip, Total, the Japanese and Phillips (an American petroleum company). Shell-BP were already joint owners of the existing Nigerian Petroleum Refinery Company Ltd (NPRC) in Port Harcourt, in which the ownership structure was Shell (25 %), BP (25 %) and the federal government (50 %). Nigeria now has located four refineries: two near Port Harcourt, one in Warri and one in Kaduna, with a total production capacity of 445,000 barrels per day. Each refinery is a wholly owned subsidiary of the Nigerian National Petroleum Corporation (NNPC).

The refinery located in Kaduna was initially conceived to be at Warri, but during the consideration of the construction, political interest was allowed to influence the change of the project location, although sound economic judgement was overwhelmingly against Kaduna. In the final analysis, building the refinery in Kaduna meant that crude oil would have to be pumped from the Niger Delta, where oil exploration took place, to Kaduna hundreds of miles away from the production point.

The two refineries located near Port Harcourt are operated as a single unit, but are regarded as separate entities. They are unable to produce at full capacity because of sabotage, fire, poor management by the NNPC and lack of regular maintenance. These problems contribute to a production output less than 300,000 barrels per day. As a result, the largest oil producer in sub-Saharan Africa has to import refined oil to make up for domestic consumption. Full utilization of the full capacity (450,000 barrels per day) has been in the plan over a long time, but the goal has remained unrealized.

The NNPC and the government say that the retail price subsidy is hurting the development of refineries and encourages the resale of refined products on the black market. Low domestic fuel prices made it more rewarding for oil companies to export crude oil rather than feed local refineries. These problems resulted in proposing the Petroleum Industry Bill (PIB), which has caused so much controversy between the government and the international oil companies. The proposed bill aims to deregulate the downstream sector in order to promote profitability.

The Kaduna Refinery, completed in 1980 (110,000 barrels per day), was reopened in February 2010, after two years of closure, as a consequence of repeated outages. The Warri Refinery (125,000 barrels per day) is located in the southern region of the Niger Delta, but produces significantly below capacity, because of problems with storage and the transportation of products. The

PIB has stood still in the National Assembly awaiting passage, but it is now unclear whether the bill will be passed soon. Also, the removal of the petroleum subsidy, which was announced to start in January 2012, has caused turbulent controversies, with stiff opposition from labour, the civil society and the Nigerian public. What the federal government took for granted since the proposal was mentioned has turned out to be the most contentious issue among Nigerians.

The government claims that savings from the subsidy removal will be used to develop infrastructure, but Nigerians are not prepared to listen to a government which they believe is corrupt. The people argue that so much public money is stolen or wasted, and therefore, any savings from the subsidy removal will go the same road.

Ironically, the federal government says that private investors will be granted licenses to establish oil refineries, but private refineries, whose licenses are yet to be renewed, have protested angrily that ten years after they were granted licences, the Department of Petroleum Resources (DPR) has turned them to 'cash-making ventures', by making them pay over N8 million each in every other year to renew their licenses, even when they have not been able to establish. It is now being feared by investors that the country may end up not having any new refineries.[19] It was reported that only nine of the proposed refineries still have valid licenses, because the government revoked some licenses for lack of performance in 2007.[20]

---

19 Oil and Gas Infrastructure, Oil Refineries, Business Monitor International Quarter 2, 2011, 29 March 2011.
20 Marcel Mbamalu, Private Refineries Lament High Cost of Licence Renewal Ignore DPR News Highlights, The Guardian (Nigeria), 6 November 2011.

CHAPTER 12

Operators in the Industry

a. Addax Petroleum

China's Sinopec acquired Addax in June 2009. The company operates one onshore block, OML 124, located in Imo State, which has two producing oil fields – Ossu and Izombe, while an undeveloped field, Njaba, was discovered in December 2008. Addax operates offshore licences – OMLs 123, 126, 137 and OPL 291 (72.5 % interest). OML 126 and OML 137 are two contiguous blocks about 90km offshore, south of Port Harcourt. Addax also has stakes in two other offshore licences – OML 67 (12 %) and OPL 227 (40 %). Addax's major Nigerian portfolio is OML 123, the company's largest licence located offshore, about 60 km south of Calabar. This licence has nine producing fields, two undeveloped oil fields, three unappraised oil discoveries, a 35 sq km undeveloped gas discovery (Oron East), as well as several exploration prospects. The company announced that it had made an onshore oil discovery on OML 124 in January 2009, from which it is now producing about 6,000 barrels per day from the Ossu and Izombe fields, located in Imo State, which is less prone to sabotage horn attack.

b. Gazprom

The Russian gas giant, Gazprom, is keen to expand its interest in the Nigerian energy sector. In June 2008, the company said it was ready to invest up to $30 billion to develop a new gas transport pipeline system to enhance gas delivery capacity. Gazprom's breakthrough came in June 2009, when it signed a $2.5 billion agreement with NNPC, to establish a 50:50 joint venture called

Nigaz. Gazprom and Oando signed an agreement to collaborate in the development of oil and gas assets in the West African subregion.

c. Afren

Afren's operations in Nigeria constitute the core of its business. The company's focus is on reserve and production growth, with an ambitious expansion plan. To achieve this ambition, Afren has been negotiating with some major oil companies on asset acquisitions estimated to be worth $200 million. The talks have resulted in an important acquisition from Shell and Total. Afren's strength lies in the spread of exploration interests, considerable undeveloped reserves and a strong African presence. It has working interests in seven licenses in Nigeria and one in the Joint Development Zone (JDZ).

The Okoro Setu block (50 % Afren) is the only one currently producing, while Ogedeh (50 %), Ofa (32.5 %), OPL 907 (41 %) and OPL 917 (42 %) are being assessed. The company has a 40 % stake in the Ebok field, now being developed and a 28 % share in the Okwok field being explored now. Afren is the technical partner in the Okoro Setu project, located in Block OML 112, being operated by Amni International, with a 50 % stake. The first production came in June 2008, and the field is currently producing at a rate of 22,000 barrels per day.

Afren was founded in 2004, with a dream to become a leading Pan-African operator, building up impressive upstream assets in the continent. It has announced production, processing and storage in the first phase of the offshore Ebok field, having been successfully installed in February 2011. In November 2010, Afren reported that the Kwok-9 appraisal well encountered more than 10 m of net oil pay which it wishes to develop as a stand-alone or a satellite to the nearby Ebok field.

First Hydrocarbon Nigeria, Afren's indigenous subsidiary, had struck a deal in October 2010 to acquire a 45 % stake in the onshore block – OML 26. The deal acquired the stake from Shell, Total and Nigeria Agip Oil Company (NAOC). The block has two wells, with a production of about 5000 barrels of oil per day, and three undeveloped, but proven assets, which will enable Afren's production to rise to 40,000 barrels per day by 2015. In June 2010, the company struck substantial oil with the Ebok deep exploration well in the OML 69, which was drilled to a depth of 3,467 m, but the well was abandoned temporarily.

In January 2010, Afren went into a joint venture with Oriental Energy, the Anglo-Norwegian Company and Energy Equity Resources (EER), in which Afren will participate in the exploration appraisal and development of the project located next to the Ebok Development Scheme. In November 2009, Afren and Oriental Energy announced oil discoveries with their Ebok-5 appraisal well. Tins oil discovery added to the gross oil hit in the DI and LD-IE reservoirs. The company agreed with Addax Petroleum to acquire a stake in the Okwok field off the southeast coast. The field in OML 67 is estimated to hold over 70 million barrels of recoverable reserves near the Ebok field. Afren will hold 28 % in the Okwok field, by acquiring 70 % of Addax's 40 % legal interest.

Afren and its Nigerian joint venture partner, Global Energy, signed PSCs for onshore gas fields in March 2008. The contract covers about 3,500 sq km and has blocks OPL 917 and OPL 907 in the Anambra Basin. It is estimated that there are reserves of 142 bcm of natural gas. OPL 907 contains the Akukwa gas and condensate discovery, holding volumes of up to 11.3 bcm, while OP 917 is the location of the Igbariam discovery, estimated to have about 8.5 bcm of gas and 80 million barrels of oil.

d. Chevron

Chevron's operational interests include oil production, domestic gas supply, pioneering gas-to-liquids production and deep-water exploration. The company was heavily involved in downstream oil activities until 2008, when it decided to divest from its marketing and other downstream businesses. Chevron's strengths are mature fields, deep water finds, a strong relationship with the NNPC, substantial production prospects and a leading role in gas projects and infrastructure. Its exposure to the attack-prone Niger Delta region and apparent over-dependence on its Nigerian operations is a point of weakness. It has great opportunities for output increase, an untapped huge gas export and gas-to-liquids project, large areas of unexplored acreage and a great potential for deep-water discoveries of large volumes of oil.

Chevron Nigeria Ltd. (CNL) (Chevron 40 %) operates 32 fields on 13 concessions, of about 8,900 sq kilometres, from which it produced 232,000 barrels per day in 2009. Chevron maintains a downstream presence, with a lubricants plant in Apapa, accounting for 186,000 bbl. Chevron is the operator of the offshore Agbami oil field, which is reported to hold up to billions of barrels of oil reserves. The company also has stakes in the Apra, Usan and Ukot discoveries. The Agbami field came onstream at the end of July 2008, with an initial production of 100,000 barrels per day, reaching its limit of 250,000 barrels per day of high quality crude and natural gas liquids in 2009. In 1997, Chevron established Nigeria's first gas gathering project in Escravos, producing gas, LPG and condensates. A phase 3A expansion has the capacity to increase gas processing from 2.9 bcm to 7 bcm, and boost LPG and condensate export capacity from 12,000 to 75,000 b/d. Chevron and NNPC are developing the Escravos gas-to-liquids (GTL) project to produce 34,000 b/d of diesel fuel and naphtha. The company is the leader of the West Africa Gas Project (WAGP), which transports Nigerian gas to Ghana, Benin and Togo. The project was inaugurated in November 2008, with gas flow reaching Takoradi from Lagos beach.

Chevron focuses on upstream ventures in Nigeria. Its overall capital and exploration budget for 2011 was $26 billion, and intends to put a portion of the spending in Nigeria, with particular emphasis on the development of the Usan and Agbami deep-water fields, and the construction of the Escravos gas-to-liquids complex.

e. ConocoPhillips

ConocoPhillips is a US integrated company with 20 % interests in onshore OMLS 60, 61, 62 and 63; 20 % interests in a deep-water OPL 214 and 47.5 % interest in OML 131. ConocoPhillips also has a 17 % stake in the Brass LNG project Nigeria is relatively minor to the company's overall portfolio. In 2009, ConocoPhillips produced 37,000 boe/d (net) in Nigeria out of which liquids was 19,000 b/d. The company was to explore in the OPL 214's Uge field in 2011 from where it expects between 100,000 and 120,000 barrels of oil equivalent per day of gross output after 2012.

f. China National Offshore Oil Corporation (CNOOC)

In 2006, CNOOC acquired 45 % in offshore concession OML 130 from South Atlantic Petroleum (Sapetro). The concession is about 1,295 sq km in the Niger Delta and is a deep-water block, in which Akpo field is located, and three other significant discoveries: Egina, Egina South and Preowei. In December 2006, CNOOC acquired 35 % working interest in the offshore OPL 229, a shallow-water block which was upgraded to OML 141 in 2008. Despite some encouraging discoveries, the company relinquished its share to the project operator, Emerald Energy. Under a new agreement, CNOOC keeps a 5 % stake simply as collateral for a loan to the project.

CNOOC held talks with the Nigerian government in the third quarter of 2009 to acquire stakes in 23 oil blocks, amounting to 6 billion barrels, but it is not confirmed that the move has yielded the amount of reserves targeted by the company.

g. Eni

Eni is one of the three European oil companies with a strong presence in Nigeria through its Agip arm since the emergence of oil in Nigeria. It has played an important part in Nigeria's gas efforts, with a share in the establishment of NLG project at Bonny and the Brass LNG project. Eni sees Nigeria as an important part of its upstream portfolio. It has mature assets, substantial production potential and extensive involvement in gas export projects. It has a good chance for output increase, considerable untapped gas export prospects and large unexplored territory. Eni's operation in Nigeria is conducted by the Nigerian Agip Oil Company (NAOC), in a Joint venture (JV), owned by Eni (20 %), the NNPC (60 %), ConocoPhillips (20 %) and Nigerian Agip Exploration (NAE).

Nigerian Agip Oil Company operates four main offshore blocks on OML 60, 61, 62 and 63. Other assets at the production and development stages include OML 125 (Eni 85 %), which came onstream in April 2004 and produced about 9000 barrels per day in 2008. Eni has a 12.5 % stake in OML 118, which holds the Bonga field. Eni also has service contracts for OML 116 (Agbara) and OML 119, which contains the Okono/Okpoho field, with about 21,000 barrels per day in 2008. Eni also has a 40 % share in OML 120 and 121, with an output capacity of 40,000 barrels per day. Eni is involved in the Shell Petroleum Development Company (SPDC) Joint Venture, in which it has 31 onshore blocks (5 % held by Eni) and five conventional offshore blocks (12.86 % held by Eni). The company has a 10.4 % share in the NLNG consortium with the NNPC, Shell and Total, and is a member of the Brass River LNG consortium to the tune of 17 %. Eni has doubled its investment in Nigeria, but is concerned about the industry reform – Petroleum Industry Bill. The company started production at the Oyo field in OML 120 in December 2009. The oil is processed via the Armada Perdana vessel, with a maximum capacity of 40,000 barrels per day and a storage capacity of one million barrels of crude oil.

h. ExxonMobil

ExxonMobil produces about 18 % of Nigeria's oil. The company holds a 40 % stake in a joint venture with NNPC on five leases, in the shallow offshore waters of south-eastern Nigeria. Exxon is a participant in Bonga field, which is operated by Shell and the East Area (AOR) Oil Recovery Scheme. The company has interests in six deep-water blocks of 12, 500 sq km, including OPL 209 (56.25 %) site of the Erha field, and Bosi development; OML 118 (20 %), containing the Bonga and Bonga north-west discoveries; Bonga South West (16 %); OPL 219 (20 %), Bolia field; OPL 220 (47.5 %), Chota discovery; and OPL 220 (30 %), Usan discovery. ExxonMobil also has a major presence in the Joint Development Zone (JDZ), which is believed to hold 6–14 bbl of oil reserves in 23 blocks in the Gulf of Guinea.

By a stroke of providence, ExxonMobil's Nigerian facilities are situated outside the Niger Delta region, free from the risk of militant attack by MEND. ExxonMobil invested about $10 billion between 2007 and 2010, to increase its crude oil production from about 600,000 barrels per day to 1,000,000 barrels per day. The company devoted $3 billion of the investment to gas projects, including the seventh train at the Bonny Island LNG project.

ExxonMobil secured a 20-year renewable extension of three shallow-water licences in November 2009. The company has operated the OMLs 67, 68 and 70 since 1968, as part of a joint venture with the NNPC. Production from the three blocks in Oso, Ekpe, Edop and Ubit oil fields is about 580,000 barrels per day. The company commenced production at its NGL facility in July 2008, operated by its subsidiary, Mobil Producing Nigeria (51 %). It is expected to recover some 275 million bbl of NGL from associated gas produced from blocks 67, 68 and 70. The project is expected to produce 50,000 barrels per day of NGL.

An offshore liquid extraction complex, a new onshore fractionation facility at Bonny Island, and an export complex linked by new pipelines process the gas into commercial products. The East Area NGL II is a follow-up to the successful start-up of the East Area Additional Oil Recovery project in June 2006. Apart from being used to produce NGL, ExxonMobil injects the associated gas recovered into the existing hydrocarbon reservoirs to enhance recovery and production. The company has established a strong presence in mature assets, substantial production prospects and extensive deep-water exploration. But it faces increasing costs in deep-water oil production. The future outlook is good for the company because it has large unexplored territory and potential for significant deep-water discoveries.

i. Oando

Originally established as a fuel importer and retailer, the company has recently embarked on expansion efforts to build up an oil services business, with investments in the upstream sector. Oando is set to invest up to $1.3 billion to enhance its upstream ambition. The company is anticipating improved prospects in the provisions in the impending Petroleum Industry Bill, which may help it to secure 300 million barrels of reserves and 100,000 barrels per day in a space of four years. In mid-October 2009, Oando got approval to enter the Akepo field (OML 90) in the shallow waters of the Niger Delta. The company took 75 % working interest in Exile Resources and 40 % share of the license. On October 19, 2009, Oando signed an agreement with Gazprom to work together in the development of oil and gas assets in the West African subregion. In February 2008, Oando acquired Shell's 49.8 % stakes in two offshore licenses, OML 125 and OML 134, becoming the first Nigerian company to secure oil production assets from any international major in Nigeria.

j. Sinopec

Sinopec secured a PSC on Block 2 in the JDZ offshore Nigeria and Sao Tome and Principe in 2006. It reported its first oil discovery in July 2010, the Udele-3 to be drilled in Block 137.

k. Korea National Oil Corporation (KNOC)

KNOC, Korea Electric Power and DAEWOO shipbuilding were awarded 60 % stake in block OPL 312 and OPL 232 in March 2006 as a consortium. The licenses were revoked in January 2009, but a court ruled that the revocation was not valid and, thus, returned the licenses to KNOC.

l. Septa Energy

Septa Energy is a Nigerian subsidiary of the UK-based, Seven Energy, which holds stakes in the Uquo field (OML 13), the Stabb Greek field (OPL 276), the Matsogo field (OML 56), the Ukana field (OPL 236) and oil mining leases 4, 38 and 41. Septa is equipped and set to undertake a multi-phase domestic gas project that will make the company the first private Nigerian company to supply gas to an independent power plant. The first phase of the project involves an investment on developing two of its gas fields and building a 60-km gas pipeline to deliver gas to Ibom Power Plant and other independent power plants in the south-east.

m. ONGC Mittal Energy (OMEL)

The India-based company, a joint venture between OVL and Mittal Investment, signed a memorandum of understanding (MoU) in November 2005, in which OMEL accepted to invest about $6 billion in infrastructure in exchange for access to exploration blocks. The investment is linked to the hydrocarbon production of 650,000 barrels of oil equivalent (boe) per day, over a duration of 25 years, implying that OMEL has agreed to invest about $1 billion in infrastructure for every barrel of oil equivalent produced.

In 2009, the NNPC approved the construction of a refinery for OMEL to refine 180,000 barrels per day in Nigeria. This development was reported to be at a cost of $4 billion. Information is not available on the location of the refinery and when it will come onstream.

n. Petrobras

Petrobras is focused on making Nigeria its most important interest outside Brazil, with Nigeria's offshore acreage providing the opportunity for the company to utilize its deep-water skills. The company's plan is to spend about $2 billion on oil exploration and production between 2009 and 2013. Petrobras entered the Nigerian upstream segment in 1998. It has an operating stake in OPL 315, and a non-operating stake in OML 127 in the Agbami field and OML 130 (20 %), where Total-operated Akpo field came onstream in 2009. Both productions from the Agbami (Petrobrai 13 %) and Akpo fields add 65,000 barrels of oil equivalent per day to Petrobras' overseas output. In September 2005, Petrobras said that the deep-water block, OPL 315, was expected to yield as much oil and gas as the nearby Bonga, Erha and Abo fields. Petrobras is the project lead operator with stake of 45 %, Statoil 45 % and 10 % for a local company.

o. BG Group

BG Group has major interests in two deep-water exploration licences and is actively involved in all of Nigeria's LNG projects as a customer of the Brass and NLNG projects. BG holds a 45 % stake in OPL 332; 66 % interest in OPL 286-DG; and 45 % stake in OPL

284-DO. BG acquired its first upstream asset in January 2006, and its second exploration asset in March 2006, by signing PSC and MoU with the NNPC for block OPL 286-DO near the Bonga field. BG took its first delivery of Nigerian LNG in January 2006, under a 20-year agreement for 2.3 million tonnes per annum from the NLNG Trains 4 and 5 located in Bonny Island. In 2007, BG signed a 20-year SPA for another 2.25 million tonnes per annum from NLNG Train 7. In July 2006, BG, NNPC and other companies signed a $6 billion LNG agreement with Olokola, NNPC (49.5 %), Chevron (18.5 %) Shell (18.5 %) and BG Group (13.5 %).

p. Shell Petroleum Development Company (SPDC)

Shell is the largest and oldest company in the Nigerian oil industry among the international oil companies. The proposed sale of some marginal assets may enhance its position in terms of reduced risk and improved profitability. The company has suffered considerably on account of its activities in the Niger Delta due to constant attack by militant groups, with resultant intermittent production disruptions. It has considerable potential from its expansive liquefied natural gas export project in the Bonny axis of the Niger Delta. Shell's offshore activities are focused largely on the Bongo project and deep-water PSC in OPL 245. Shell's strengths are its established presence in mature assets, its good relationship with the NNPC, substantial production potential and involvement in gas export projects. However, some of its weaknesses are limitations in deep-water exploration, over-dependence on Nigeria in group portfolio and high-risk capital commitment. But it has an abundance of opportunities in large areas of unexplored territory, enormous untapped gas export potential and scope for significant output rise with the OPEC change of policy.

The Shell Petroleum Development Company (SPDC) Joint Venture pumps about 900,000 to 1,000,000 barrels of crude oil per day, accounting for about 33 % of Nigeria's total crude output, although its installed capacity is at 1.3 million barrels per day. The SPDC's Joint Venture reserves are thought to be about 53 % of Nigeria's total reserves. Shell holds a 30 % interest in the joint venture, while NNPC, Total and Eni have 55 %, 10 % and 5 %, respectively.

In 1998, Shell established Shell Gas, which operates two gas distribution projects as part of the company's commitment to end gas flaring. Shell is the technical adviser to the Nigerian Liquefied Natural Gas at Bonny Island, with a 25.6 % shareholding, to which the partners (including NNPC, Total and Eni) have committed $21 billion in investment. Shell Gas has signed agreements to purchase 3 million tonnes per annum of LNG from the sixth train, with Total to purchase one million tonnes per annum. It was reported that eighteen consortia were preparing bids for Shell's onshore Nigerian assets to be relinquished. The assets are said to include OMLs 26, 30, 34, 40 and 42. Shell attributes the decision to its concern that Nigeria would be unlikely to fund its share of the joint venture projects, but also admits that it also faces considerable security problems onshore.[21] Shell's onshore Gbaran-Ubie integrated project came onstream in July 2010, to produce 10.3 billion cubic meters of gas plus 70,000 barrels of oil and condensate. Gbaran-Ubie is one of the first Nigerian upstream projects to utilize its full associated gas production, complying with the gas flaring regulation under the Nigerian Gas Master Plan. In May 2010, Shell said it was hoping to invest $2 billion in projects that will cut its gas flaring in the Niger Delta by 75 %. The projects will entail upgrading, replacing the existing associated-gas gathering (AGG) facilities or installing new facilities where they are non-existent. By 29 January 2010, Shell had sold its 30 % interest in licenses 4, 38 and 41 to a consortium of Nigerian and foreign companies. The licenses, covering about 2,650 sq. kilometres in the west of the Niger Delta, were sold to Seplat Petroleum and Shebah Petroleum Company consortium, and Maurel and Prom of France.

---

21 Nigeria Oil and Gas Report, Quarter 3, Business Monitor International Ltd., 2011, pp. 75–113

q. Total

Total acquired Elfin 1999, making the company a major investor in Nigeria. It plays a major role in the NLNG export programme and has established a strong position in mature oil production. It has mature assets and deep-water promise, with a substantial production increase potential for the future. Its fortunes lie in its large untapped gas export, considerable unexplored fields, and prospects for deep water huge discoveries. The company operates through Elf Petroleum Nigeria (EPN), a 40:60 joint venture between Total and the NNPC. It has operating stakes in OML 58 (40 %), OML 99 (30.4 %), OML 100 (40 %) and OML 102 (40 %). Additionally, Total has a 12.5 % stake in deep-water OML 118, the site of the Bonga oil field.

In the downstream sector, the company has a retail network of about 525 service stations across Nigeria. It also has a 15 % interest in the NLNG project. Total's Amenam-Kpono fields produced about 125,000 barrels per day in 2004, one year after the fields came onstream. It holds a 20 % stake in OPL 222, which EPN operates in the site of the Usan and Ukot discoveries. The company currently invests about $7 billion on four projects, which include the Usan deep-water offshore field and the OML 58 license in the Niger Delta.

In July 2010, Total bought Chevron's 45.9 % stake in the Joint Development Zone Block I, covering 700 sq kilometres in water. The company is working as the operator, with Dangote Energy Equity Resources and Sasol Production Nigeria. The licence is valid until 2046. Total and Conoil Producing discovered hydrocarbons with the Agge-3B.T1 well in OML 136 in 2010, where it holds 40 % stake and Conoil, the operator of the well, holds 60 %.

The Akpo field, operated by Total, came onstream in March 2009 from OML 130, situated 200 km offshore from Port Harcourt Total has a 24 % stake in the project, while the other partners are CNOOC (45 %) and Petrobras (20 %). Total announced the discovery at the Etisong field of OML 102 in December 2008, which is being developed by a Total/NNPC Joint Venture. Total Exploration and

Production Nigeria started its OML 58 upgrade project in October 2008, where it has a 40 % operating interest located onshore in Rivers State, about 85 kilometres northwest of Port Harcourt and the NNPC holds 60 % stake in the project. The OML 58 development project is aimed at increasing gas production capacity from 3.87 bcm to 5.69 bcm, and increase oil and condensate output by about 15,000 b/d, to bring the total output to 140,000 barrels of oil equivalent per day.[22] The company has acquired a 40 % stake in OML 136 and Conoil Production will retain the 60 % balance in the field. By acquiring Chevron's 17 % interest in the Brass LNG project in 2006, Total added to its presence in Nigeria substantially.

r. Nigerian National Petroleum Corporation (NNPC)

The Nigerian National Petroleum Corporation (NNPC) is vested with exclusive responsibility for upstream and downstream development, which covers exploiting, refining and marketing of Nigeria's crude oil. The NNPC supervises and overseas government investments in the industry through the National Petroleum Investment Management Services (NAPIMS). All NNPC upstream operations are managed under the Exploration and Production Directorate, which include the following strategic business units (SBUs) operating directly under the NNPC:
- National Petroleum Investment Management Services (NAPIMS)
- Eleme Petrochemicals Company
- Crude Oil Sales Division (COSD)
- Integrated Data Services Limited (IDSL)
- Nigerian Petroleum Development Company (NPDC)
- Pipelines and Products Marketing Company (PPMC)
- Nigerian Gas Company (NGC)

---

22 Nigeria Oil and Gas Report, Quarter 2, Business Monitor International Ltd., 2011.

These SBUs are collectively responsible for surveys, seismic data collation and interpretation, crude oil exploration, production, transportation, storage and marketing. The downstream operations cover crude oil/gas conversion into refined and petrochemical products, gas treatment, as well as the transportation and marketing of petroleum products.

The downstream plants under the NNPC include the four refineries, with a total installed capacity of 445,000 barrels per day – two in Port Harcourt (210,000 barrels per day), one each in Warri and Kaduna (125,000 and 110,000 barrels per day, respectively). The three petrochemical plants in Warri, Kaduna and Eleme, and some gas projects are part of the downstream operations. Nigeria has 5000 kilometres of pipeline network, with 21 storage depots and 9 LPG depots. In 2008, the oil and gas sector reform implementation committee was set up to make far-reaching proposals on how to reform the industry, with particular focus on re-engineering the NNPC, which has become notorious for poor performance and corruption. A Petroleum Industry Bill (PIB) has been in the National Assembly since 2007. The decision to fragment the structure of the NNPC is aimed at enhancing its operational ability to perform well. This is exhaustively treated in the chapter on the industry reform.

CHAPTER 13

A Comparative Picture of the Oil Companies

The government window on the oil industry is the Nigerian National Petroleum Corporation (NNPC), which provides about 50 % of crude oil, 40 % of natural gas supply and 100 % of oil refining. The international oil companies are major partners with the NNPC, through the profit sharing contract (PSC) option. Shell is the largest foreign investor in Nigeria (about 15 % of Shell's total global oil output). It has 26 % of NLNG gas export project and is heavily involved in major development projects. ExxonMobil produced about 39,000 barrels per day in 2009. Key projects include the Yoho and Erha fields and participation in Bonga.

Chevron's net oil output in 2009 was an average of 232,000 b/d, with a gas production of 0.5 bcm. Major development projects include the Agbami field, the Olokola LNG scheme, the West Africa Gas Pipeline and the Escravos Gas-to-Liquids plant with Sasol. Eni holds 15 % of NLNG and has 100 % of the deep-water OPL 221 Production Sharing Contracts (DSC). Eni holds 10 % of NLNG gas export and is a member of the Brass LNG Consortium. Its net production in 2009 was 90,000 b/d of oil and 2.2 bcm of gas.

Total has a 15 % stake in NLNG, 100 % of the deep-water Oil Prospecting Licence 221 and Production Sharing Contract. It acquired Chevron's 17 % share in the Brass LNG in 2006. Total pumped 159,000 barrels per day of crude oil and 3.9 bcm of gas in 2009. The Akpo field, in which Total has a 24 % operating share, came onstream in March 2009, with the hope of producing the equivalent of 175,000 barrels of oil per day. Total is reported to have replaced Chevron in the offshore Joint Development Zone (JDZ) shared by Nigeria and Sao Tome and Principe, by acquiring Chevron's 45.9 % stake.

ConocoPhillips pumped 19,000 barrels per day of Nigerian crude in 2009 and 1.2 bcm of gas production, leading to 39,000 boe/d of hydrocarbon output. ConocoPhillips is a partner in the Brass LNG project.

The UK-based BG Group agreed to buy 2 million tpa of LNG from the Brass project. It also acquired a 45 % stake in offshore block 332, as operator of the licence, in collaboration with Sahara Energy Exploration. It is a partner in the Olokola LNG Scheme. In February 2007, the group BG signed a 20-year sale and purchase agreement (SPA) for 2.25 tpa from the NLNG's Train 7 and a PSC for Block OPL 286 – DO with NNPC.

Afren announced in October 2010 that its subsidiary, First Hydrocarbon Nigeria (FHN), had struck a deal to acquire a 45 % stake in Oil Mining Licence 26 onshore from Shell, Total and Nigeria Agip Oil Company (NAOC). Afren hopes its production will increase to 40,000 b/d by the year 2015.

Petrobras expected the deep-water block OPL 315 to yield as much oil and gas as the nearby Bonga, Erha, and Abo fields. Petrobras holds a 20 % stake in the Akpo field and is set to invest about $2 billion on oil exploration and production between 2009 and 2013.

CHAPTER 14
Production Outlook

Nigeria was reported to have proven oil reserves of 37.2 billion barrels by the end of 2009 in the *BP Statistical Review of World Energy and Oil and Gas Journal* (OGJ).[23] The Nigerian government had hoped to increase the figure to 40 billion barrels by 2010, but the figure had dropped to 31.8 billion barrels by August 2010.[24] The bulk of the reserves are found along the Niger Delta, with most of the oil located in hundreds of sub-50 million barrel fields. There are many similar fields, whose reserves have not been fully disclosed. In addition, there are deep-water and ultra-deep-water oil prospects off the coast.

Crude oil production by September 2010 was reported to be 2.15 million barrels per day, as against the estimated production capacity of 2.25 million barrels (International Energy Agency). The reported shortfall in production witnessed in recent years was as a result of Shell's shutdown of its Forcados terminal, with about 550,000 barrels of oil lost as a result of militant attacks on Eni's and Chevron's facilities, which disrupted oil flows.

Some consortia are reported to be interested in bids for offshore leases to be surrendered by Shell. Some of the companies mentioned in the consortia include Russia's Gazprom, Seplat Petroleum and the Niger Delta Petroleum Resources. Afren announced that its Nigerian arm had decided to buy stakes from Shell, Total and Eni. First Hydrocarbon Nigeria, with a 45 % holding by Afren, agreed to buy a 45 % stake in OML 26, containing two producing fields and three undeveloped assets.[25]

---

23 BP Statistical Review of World Energy, June 2010.
24 Oil and Gas Journal (OGJ), December 2010.
25 Nigeria Oil and Gas Report. Quarter 2, 2011; Reportlinker, 7 April 2011.

In 2010, Nigeria formally requested that OPEC should review the allocation of targets which was done in September 2008, stating that Nigeria was entitled to a larger quota. It was argued, by Nigeria, that when OPEC set the quota, her output was lower than normal as a result of the Niger Delta attacks which caused disruptions in production. Historically, Nigeria's production capacity gave her 8 % in OPEC quota, but the allocation fell to 6.7 %. Nigeria seems to have overcome the problems which impeded development in the oil sector and the country has returned to higher production levels, with the possibility of even higher production. African oil output was about 9.98 million barrels per day in 2010, and it was predicted that it may rise to about 11.9 million barrels by 2015. This forecast appears to be in danger of not being realized with the developments taking place in some African countries.

In November 2010, Afren announced the discovery of Okwok-9, with a capacity of about 25 million barrels of oil. Oil production in Nigeria rose from 2.15 million barrels per day in September 2010 to 2.28 million barrels per day by December 2010. Damaged infrastructures were repaired, leading to increased output in Qua Iboe crude and Bonny light, but militants attacked critical pipelines in late December 2010. The volume of Bonny light is expected to increase with the completion of the new Nembe Creek/Trunk line, which will convey about 600,000 barrels per day of crude oil from 14 flow stations in the Niger Delta to the Bonny Export Terminal.[26]

Total announced that its deep-water Usan field will start production in 2012. When it is launched, Usan will produce about 180,000 barrels of oil per day. Usan is located in license OML 138, in which Total has a 20 % stake.

Afren expects to produce over 15,000 barrels per day from a first phase development of its Ebok field in OML 67 block offshore. This production was expected in February 2011.

---

[26] M. Clark, Nigeria Coming of Age. Petroleum Economist Euromoney Institutional Investors Plc, London, October 2006. 94

Interest in Nigeria's deep-water acreage increased in recent years. Abo field, operated by Agip, was the only deep-water producer in water depths of about 800 meters. But Bonga field, operated by Shell's SNEPCO, came on-stream nearly one decade after its discovery in the 1990s. The Bonga field, which produces about 205,000 barrels per day, cost a whopping $3.6 billion. The first shipment of Bonga crude marked a new era for Nigeria's oil, and gas industry. There is great potential for growth because the offshore sector is still far from being fully explored.

Bonga was followed a few months later by Erha, under the joint operation of ExxonMobil and Shell in Block 209, in water depths of 1,200 metres and producing 150,000 barrels per day, with the Erha North satellite field producing 40,000 barrels per day.

Shell Nigeria Exploration and Production Company's logistics base in Snake Island, Lagos, has become a support centre for the deep-water industry to grow. There is a cluster of facilities being built by other oil companies as capacity-building outfits to support the industry.

Over the next few years, barring unforeseen disruptions, deep-water output is predicted to rise. ExxonMobil's 120,000 barrels per day from Bosi field has started up, followed by Chevron's Agbami and Shell's Bonga Southwest project, which add 450,000 barrels per day. Total's Akpo field and Usan/Ukot field add about 400,000 barrels per day. These deep-water productions confirm Nigeria as a world-class deep-water producer. Although there were unavoidable delays to the start-up dates of some of the projects, their successful development may become the surest way to realize Nigeria's output target of about 4 million barrels per day.

In May 2006, ExxonMobil discovered Ugo-1 in oil production licence (OPL) 214, about 113 kilometres offshore in a string of deep-water fields. This field is in a water depth of 1,283 metres, about 145 kilometres southeast of Erha. In 2005, Shell discovered the Etan-IX in Block OPL 245 at 1,720 meters of water depth, and Bobo IX in block OPL 322 at 2,479 meters, perhaps one of the deepest wells known. Close to Shell's Bonga Southwest is Chevron's Aparo discovery in 1,245 meters of water.

New investors are showing interest because of the potential reserves. Deep-water exploration was dominated by the deep pocket multinationals, notably ExxonMobil, Total, Chevron and Shell. But, state-owned Asian investors are now in the field, including India's Oil and Gas Corporation, Korea's National Oil Corporation (KNOC), and China's CNOOC, which paid $2.3 billion for a 40 % share of the Akpo field.

Nigeria is most likely to account for about 8.82 % of the African regional oil demand by 2015, while she will provide 23.07 % of supply.[27]

Deep-water development is costly and risky, but it has great potential reward for investors. The potential for uninterrupted production is high because of the remote locations offshore. The Nigerian National Petroleum Corporation (NNPC) has indicated that it intends to take over the operation of four oil blocks being sold by Shell, a decision that has generated worry among oil companies buying the blocks from Shell. It was strange that the NNPC, owner of 55 % of the blocks, announced in June 2010 that companies that had bought blocks OML 30, 34, 40 and 42 should not assume that they would become the operators. The blocks, NNPC indicated, would be operated by NNPC's subsidiary, the Nigerian Petroleum Development Company, which currently produces 100,000 barrels per day.

It is difficult to judge the success of the amnesty scheme so far. Despite the large army of militants who signed up for the scheme and reduction of attacks on oil installations, some militants still operate in the creeks. In June 2011, a faction of the Movement for the Emancipation of the Niger Delta (MEND), who did not embrace the amnesty offer, threatened to attack Eni, an Italian company. MEND's present militancy capacity is unclear, but

---

27 Nigeria Oil and Gas Report, Quarter 2, 2011; Reportlinker, 7 April 2011.

since the issues fuelling the crisis are still largely unresolved, local warlords and ambitious commanders may find recruitment easy.

So far, there is no proof that the amnesty scheme has had a permanent effect on curbing the activities of criminal gangs who operate for personal gain. For example, Shell had to declare *a force majeure* on its Bonny light loading for June and July 2011, cutting back production due to leaks and fires on one pipeline. The damage was caused by oil saboteurs, whose motive was to steal oil. However, the amnesty programme has brought some stability and enabled an environment for noticeable increases in oil and gas production.

By the middle of 2011, in the face of minimum disruption to drilling and oil production, oil companies were showing signs of competitive pursuit of investments in deep-water and in the petrochemical sector. Total announced that production from its Usan field will commence in 2012, with an estimated production of 180,000 barrels of oil equivalent per day. Usan deep-water field is in OML 138, in which Total holds a 20 % operating share. Afren planned to produce over 15,000 barrels per day from the first phase of development of their Ebok field in the OML 67 block, beginning from February 2011. From the outlook of production, it was considered possible to see a production average of 2.75 million barrels per day before the end of 2012, although the output forecast was 2.40 million barrels per day.

Chevron's Agbami project is one of the largest deep-water discoveries in Nigeria. The field was discovered in 1998, with an estimated 900 million barrels of oil. The first oil production was in 2008, and the initial oil equivalent production rapidly climbed to more than 110,000 barrels per day, which rose up to 250,000 barrels per day by the end of 2009. The discovery is in OPL 216, in depths ranging from 1,280 to 1,646 metres, making it the deepest project in Nigeria. Development drilling and completion operation started in 2006 and the subsea installation of production equipment began the following year. Chevron operates the project on a 68 % stake along with **NNPC**, Famfa Oil, Petrobras and Statoil.

Barring unforeseen difficulties from sabotage, theft, corruption and political instability, experts agree that the production outlook is bright for Nigeria's oil and gas. Observers forecast that oil and gas production should increase by about 50 % by 2020, with gas production rising to 80 bcm, while export potential should rise to 39 bcm. The federal government has indicated that it will clean up the economy, help the oil and gas sector to rise to its full potential, and put an end to the era of corruption and inefficiency. Officials admit that the nation's natural resources earnings have been squandered in the past, but that this has to change by modernizing the downstream sector and reducing environmental damage. The department of petroleum resources also aims to increase crude reserves significantly and to boost production capacity.

CHAPTER 15
The Natural Gas Question

It was estimated that Nigeria's natural gas reserves are three times her crude oil reserves. About 3000 million standard cubic feet of gas is produced annually, a small portion of which is re-injected into reservoirs to enhance the recovery of crude oil. The greatest part of what is produced is thus flared in the process of drilling for crude oil. Only recently were efforts made by oil companies to exploit the enormous gas produced for commercial purposes. In 1988, the NNPC set up a company, the Nigerian Gas Company, with the task of developing, harnessing and marketing natural gas in the local market. In consequence of the concern over this wastage, the gas/oil ratio (GOR) was devised after the example of the Oil and Gas Conservation Board in Canada, where they adopt cost-effective and resource utilization strategies, with the efficient production and full commercialization of products.

In 1964/65, the Canadian government sponsored a gas utilization study, which sent a small team to Nigeria. The team recommended that gas could be piped to Lagos for the Electricity Corporation of Nigeria at a cost of $12 million. That proposition was aborted because the World Bank did not want a rival project that would affect its sponsored project, the Kainji Dam Project.

Another attempt was made in 1966/67, when Shell-BP intended to establish a Liquefied National Gas Plant. That attempt failed also. Thus, for a very long time, Nigeria has flared more natural gas than any oil-producing country, with estimates suggesting that about 70 % is flared, a situation which points to the inertia and weakness of the country to enforce the repeated policy against flaring.

The common reason for the inexcusable waste is always that in order to maximize the production of crude oil, the associated gas must be burned off. It is ironic that natural gas is also extracted for commercial purposes where it is found in isolation. This is known as non-associated gas. The oil companies say that it is costly to separate commercially profitable associated gas from the oil. Thus, the associated gas found with oil must be disposed of by burning off to increase crude oil production. This is absolutely against the economy, but it has continued for decades without the moral force to stop the practice.

Gas flaring started since the emergence of oil extraction by Shell-BP. Britain believed that the practice was bad, but gas flaring continued with no practical efforts towards the cessation of the practice. This contrasts sharply with oil exploration in much of Europe, Britain not exempted, where associated gas is used or re-injected into the ground. Gas flaring anywhere is discouraged because it is known to cause climate change.

The consequences of gas flaring are becoming increasingly obvious in southern Nigeria, where oil exploration is concentrated. Gas flaring is known to release large amounts of methane, which is known to have very high global warning consequences. The methane is accompanied by carbon dioxide, of which oil exploration was calculated to have caused over 30,000,000 tonnes in 2002. Thus, as flaring diminishes elsewhere, it has increased here in proportion to the increase in oil production, which is pursued vigorously by the oil companies with the support of a country in dire need of the revenue from oil. Because of an amazing appetite for higher production on the part of the producers and the inertia of the ruling class, gas flaring has continued unabated, even with the 1984 Associated Gas Reinjection Act in its section 3.

The reason is found in the level of greed and corruption in the Nigerian oil and gas sector. No one can truthfully claim to know exactly how much gas is flared even today, because there is a pervasive culture of connivance between the oil companies and the corrupt public officials in charge of the oil sector. For instance, the oil companies claim that only 50 % of all associated gas is burnt off, but only a few accept this figure.

Just as oil brought enormous fortunes to Nigeria, there is ample evidence that much damage has been inflicted on the country, in terms of the bad effects of oil production and the level of waste and corruption brought by the wealth accruing from oil and gas. The people of Delta State live in abject poverty as their environment is destroyed, eroding farming and fishing prospects. It is a paradox that more than 70 % of the people of the Niger Delta region live in poverty. The result of such a situation is the incidence of militancy sponsored against government in the agitation for improved conditions in the region.

The natural gas question is not only limited to the issue of gas gathering for consumption, but also concerns the wastage of gas and its consequences. Improved utilization of gas, instead of flaring, is a means of reducing global carbon emissions. Gas flaring is responsible for the vast majority of both wasted energy and greenhouse gas emissions. It was estimated that the total gas flaring over a fifteen-year period generated about 5,000 mega metric tonnes of carbon dioxide or roughly about 70 % of the total annual greenhouse gas emissions of the United States in 2007.

Nigeria's oil wealth has been exploited for more than 50 years, but while the oil-producing companies have profited from the oil, local communities in the oil region live with the pollution caused by gas flaring. In Western Europe, more than 90 % of associated gas is used or re-injected into the ground. In Nigeria, in spite of regulations introduced more than twenty years ago, much of the associated gas is flared, the effect of which is pollution and climate change. Information suggests that over 3.5 billion standard cubic feet (scf) of associated gas was produced in 2000, of which 70 % was flared.[28] As oil production increased, Nigeria became one of the biggest gas flaring, oil-producing nations, with about 2 million standard cubic feet (scf) flared daily. This was estimated to be about 25 % of UK's gas consumption.

Nigeria's annual revenue loss due to flaring is about $2.5 billion. The practice has been advanced to an alarming level by

---

28 Media Briefing. Gas Flaring in Nigeria. Friends of the Earth, October 2004 (www.foe.co.uk/resource/media_briefing/gasflaringinniger pdf)

Shell, ExxonMobil, Chevron, Texaco, Agip and TotalFinElf, in joint ventures with the Nigerian National Petroleum Corporation. This is clearly strange, since this practice has been made illegal since 1984, in consequence of a section of the Associated Gas Reinjection Act of 1979.

The first attempt at forcing oil companies to end gas flaring was in 1969, when the administration of Yakubu Gowon ordered them to install facilities that would utilize associated gas within five years of commencing operations in Nigeria. After five years, the companies did not keep faith with that order. The deadline was moved to 1979. Another failure by the oil companies to meet the new date led to yet a new date of 1984, but this time, a fine was to be paid by defaulters. The federal government again pledged to end gas flaring by January 2008 and the date was again changed to 31 December 2008. Why were these delays experienced? Until recently, the market for gas in Nigeria was limited and there was no economical method to ship it to overseas markets. Today, it is possible for gas to be liquefied and shipped to major markets. Oil companies, led by Shell, have invested in terminals to ship liquefied natural gas.

An end to the flaring is needed badly, not merely for the health of Nigeria's economy, but also for the health of the people. The shutdown of the supply of national gas to Bonny Island Liquefied Natural Gas (LNG) plant in early December 2008 is the consequence of the long drawn struggle between the people of the oil-producing region, the federal government and the oil companies. The abrupt termination of supply from the Shell Petroleum Development Company's Soku upstream plant came at a time of controversy over repeatedly breached deadlines for ending of flaring.[29]

With the construction of several LNG export facilities and the West African Gas Pipeline (WAGP), Nigeria is beginning to realize its gas development potential. It was estimated that Nigeria's annual liquefied natural gas (LNG) capacity could in-

---

29 The Global Oil and Gas Industry, (www.oilgasarticles.com).

crease from 30 billion cubic meters in 2008 to 70 billion cubic metres by 2011.[30] Gasprom, Russian gas export monopoly confirmed early in 2011 that it was in active talks with the Nigerian government to develop her vast natural gas reserves. Royal Dutch Shell Pic has also signed an agreement for a pipeline project worth $101 million. The contract with Saipem Contracting Nigeria covers 42 kilometres for the purpose of gathering gas for domestic use in Nigeria.[31]

The continued flaring of gas is no longer excusable, because it can no longer be attributed to the inadequate capacity to process the gas, or the high capital cost of associated gas gathering and limited domestic demand. Capacity is rising and domestic demand is increasing, but if the capacity utilization does not outpace demand, the opportunity for catching up in the market may be lost as a direct consequence. Long-term structural and political factors will continue to hold back the Nigerian oil and gas industry. One of the many problems facing the industry is the lack of competitively priced feedstock supplies.

While Nigeria is beginning to tap into its potential in natural gas, which can serve as an important source of competitively priced feedstock, the refinery arm of the sector is still unable to process the nation's crude output. The combined production capacity of the refineries in Port Harcourt, Warri and Kaduna is less than 25 % of crude oil production. Problems facing full-capacity utilization include sabotage, fire, poor management and political instability. In 2008, oil production fell to around 1.5 million barrels per day. Some petrochemical projects were planned in recent years, which had to be cancelled as a result of political and security problems. There is also the unresolved resistance by oil companies to government's insistence on the control of the joint venture projects. Another intractable problem is the removal of

---

30 Routers. Gas Flaring in Nigeria. Reuters, (www.ukreuters.com/at tides/2008).
31 Downstream Today. Shell signs deal for pipeline project 11 April 2011, www.downstreamtoday.com/fhf.aspx?aspxerrorpath=/news/articles.aspx.

subsidy, which oil companies have been advocating, but which has faced strong objection from the public and labour.

A promising development is the Viva Methanol (Methanol to olefini-MTO) project, which should have a great impact on the petrochemical sector. The project was scheduled to start up in 2012, with a capacity for 1.3 million tonnes per annum of methanol and 400,000 tonnes of polypropylene. Some experts have doubts that the project will come on stream before 2013, judging from Nigeria's past performance in handling large petrochemical projects. Poor infrastructure, political problems, labour objection, sabotage, poor management, and large-scale corruption remain barriers to investments, which raise the risks and initial costs of downstream projects. Although the petrochemical sector has been planning for privatization, so as to improve performance and add value to the oil and gas output, there are doubts about investor's willingness to risk their capital in where there are so many unknown potential risks.

International oil companies have proposed some large joint ventures to produce olefini and polymers, a range of aromatics, methanol and oxygenates. They wish to finance such projects if they will be allowed to control the ventures and sell their chemicals in the local market at international market prices. These conditions will result in the removal of subsidy as the public understands it, which the labour strongly objects to.

Nigeria launched a three-phase master plan in the seventies to produce a wide range of petrochemicals. Only two of the phases are operating because of delays caused by lack of funding and the failure of government to give leadership. For instance, work on the Eleme Petrochemical Plant was suspended for eight years because the government was unable to pay the heavy debts it owed the Japanese and French contractors then.

Nigeria's most ambitious gas project on Bonny Island was completed in September 1995. The 4th and 5th trains entered production in 2005. A 6th train has added 5.5 billion cubic metres to the plant's annual capacity, which brings the plant's total capacity to 31 billion cubic metres.

A memorandum of understanding (MoU) for a third LNG plant was signed between ConocoPhillips and Eni and the Nigerian government in September 2001. The plant, said to be the world's first offshore LNG plant, was scheduled to commence deliveries in 2013, but violence in the Niger Delta has caused delays to the schedule.

In January 2005, ExxonMobil signed an MoU to study the construction of a second LNG plant in Bonny Island, which was to begin functioning in 2011, with a capacity of 4.8 million tonnes per annum. The Nigerian National Petroleum Corporation, Shell and others signed an LNG agreement, covering Olokola LNG (OKLNG) project, which was also expected to come on-stream in 2011. The partners in the project were NNPC (49.5 %), Chevron (18.5 %), Shell (18.5 %) and BG Group (13.5 %). The complex is planned to produce substantial quantities of natural gas liquids as a by-product. In February 2007, Eni signed a 20-year sale and purchase agreement (SPA) with NLNG for the acquisition of 1.38 million tonnes per annum of LNG from the Train 7 expansion. Total announced that it had signed a sale and purchase agreement for the same volume of gas from Train 7. Petrobras of Brazil has signed a master agreement with NLNG for the supply of gas. Centrica, a British utility company, signed a $12 million contract to build a new LNG plant in Akwa-Ibom State.

Since 2002, a trans-Sahara gas pipeline project has been conceived to transport gas from Nigeria via Niger and Algeria to Europe at an estimated capital cost of $10 billion, and $3 billion for gathering centres. The project was planned to come onstream in 2015. On July 3, 2009, Nigeria, Algeria and Niger finalized the agreement to build the project. NNPC (Nigeria) and Sonatract (Algeria) will hold a 45 % stake each, while Niger will hold 10 %, Interests from foreign companies have heightened since the agreement was signed, with Total, Eni, Royal Dutch Shell and Gazprom showing interest to participate.

The Nigerian government had disclosed a desire to increase revenue from gas exports to 50 % of oil revenue by the year 2010, an ambition which could not be achieved. NNPC projects that about $15 billion will be required in private sector investment to realize all gas development goals. Obstacles remain strong in the way of achieving the dream. ExxonMobil began production at its natural gas liquids facility, which will recover about 275 million barrels of national gas liquids from associated gas from blocks 67, 68 and 70.

The West African Gas Pipeline (WAGP), which will transport gas from the Niger Delta through Benin Republic and Togo to Ghana, was completed in March 2007. The facilities at the Itoki Natural Gas Export terminal in Nigeria were commissioned on 28 November 2008, with the transportation of gas from Lagos Beach to Takoradi in Ghana commencing on December 5. What was tagged the 'gas revolution' was launched in March 2011, in a plan that focuses the utilization of gas as feedstock to produce low-end plastic and packaging products, as well as products such as menthol, fertilizer and other petrochemical products.

Some memoranda of understanding (MoU) were signed by the NNPC, and companies from India and Saudi Arabia. Nagarjuna, an Indian company, is expected to build two fertilizer plants at a cost of $2.5 billion; while Saudi Arabia's Natpet is to build a petrochemical plant at a cost of $3.5 billion. The petrochemical plant is to be located in Koko Free Trade Zone in Delta State, while one of the fertilizer plants would be built in Lagos and the other in Delta State.

Oando and Agip signed an agreement to invest $3 billion in a gas processing plant, for turning wet gas from oil wells into usable dry gas, for various gas end-users projects. The Oando/Agip facility would be located at Obiafu in Rivers State. It is planned that Chevron will deliver 175 million cubic feet of gas daily once the pipelines and infrastructure are ready.

In the wake of worldwide nuclear energy disasters, nations which depend on nuclear plants for energy may have to review their nuclear energy programmes. The crisis signifies a possible shift from nuclear to gas-fired turbines. This development will result in an increased demand by consumer nations for liquefied natural gas, a development which points to a positive sign for Nigeria's natural gas industry. The gas revolution and the gas-to-power tariffs previously introduced are still within the context of the gas master plan, which encompasses gas gathering production and processing, gas transmission, gas distribution and provision of gas-end-user facilities. The full implementation of the gas master plan will result in about $25 billion worth of foreign investment in gas processing, transmission and downstream gas utilization projects, which should prove Nigeria's rightful place in the global oil and gas picture, if efficiently managed. The success of this project will depend on the effective implementation of the Petroleum Industry Bill (PIB), which has been under debate for some time.

With ExxonMobil's production at its NGL facility, the East Area NGL project promises to reduce gas flaring from its blocks 67, 68, 70. Septa Energy is set to invest $1 billion in a domestic gas project, which will join in the pursuit of gas flaring reduction. Shell plans to reduce its gas flaring by 75 %. Without a doubt, Nigeria has recently made some progress in the utilization of her gas production. Gas flaring was about 42 % of gas production in 2005 compared with 28 % flared in 2009. This is, by far, still higher than international standards, but hope is rising for gas flaring reduction, going by the investment plans of Septa and Shell.

Ohimain[32] noted in 2010 that Nigeria has recently entered the bio-energy sector, by feeding the market with imported ethanol until adequate capacity exists for the production of ethanol. The Nigerian Biofuel Policy was announced in 2007, to provide for the production of bio-ethanol to meet the national need of 5.14 billion litres per annum. Some investors have responded with investments worth over $3.86 billion, in the construction of 19 ethanol bio-refineries, 10,000 units of mini-refineries and feed stocks, and plantations for the production of more than

---

32 E.I. Ohimain, Emerging bio-ethanol projects in Nigeria: Their opportunities and challenges, Energy Policy, 2010; 38 (11): 7161–7168.

2.66 billion litres of grade ethanol per year. The potential benefits of the bio-ethanol projects include investment in the economy, employment, energy generation and a boost of the rural infrastructure.

Nigeria LNG Limited (NLNG) completed its two-train 5.9 million-tonnes per year base project in 19999. The project is run by a joint venture company owned by the NNPC (49 %), Shell Gas BV (25.6 %), Cleag Ltd (Elf 15 %) and Agip International BV (10.4 %). The company was established to liquefy natural gas derived from the large gas reserves owned by three joint venture projects for the global market. The liquefaction plant is located in Finima, Bonny Island. An expansion programme was undertaken with the construction of a third LNG processing train. The scope of the expansion project includes modifications to equip the plant to process 100 % associated gas. This step allowed the monetization of a significant amount of the gas that was being flared. The plant is located on the Bonny Riverbank, where other industrial facilities such as Shell's Bonny crude oil terminal and Mobil's Oso NGL plant are located. The facility has two-train LNG plants, a 217-km gas transmission system and a residential area, the whole site being large enough to accommodate five LNG trains.

The successful completion of NLNG's base project is a major sign of progress for Nigeria, because it will help to diversify the economy, reduce gas flaring and the dependence on oil export, and develop its considerable gas reserves. The base project plant consists of two liquefaction trains, with a production capacity of 2.9 million tonnes per year (tpy). Each liquefaction train includes a refrigerant fractionation process, with full complement for the recovery of ethane and propane for refrigerant make-up purposes and condensate as a saleable by-product. The first LNG cargo was shipped in October in 1999, while the other train was put into production in February 2000. Both trains are producing at full capacity. Production, which was at 5.4 million tonnes from the two production trains in 1999, has since risen to 9 million tonnes of LNG with the installation of another train.

Export was in the region of $56 billion a year in 2009, of which over $1 billion accrued to the NNPC. By 2010, the number of trains had risen to seven and all were producing at full capacity. With the great promise in the contribution from the NLNG and the prospect of other natural gas plants upcoming, the Nigerian gas sector offers huge possibilities and challenges. It is estimated that Nigeria's gas reserves-to-production ratio is about 120 years, while its crude oil reserves-to-production ratio is about 35 years.[33] Nigeria's gas fortunes are therefore enormous and waiting to be fully tapped. Reserves are split nearly evenly between associated and non-associated gas, but exploitation has been directed towards associated gas, which accounts for 70 % of total gas production. The current policy thrust is to end gas flaring completely; consequently, several gas utilization projects have been launched, completed or are at advanced stages of implementation as observed.[34]

After many years of regrettable waste and pollution, through the flaring of natural gas, it appears that with the emergence of the NLNG and government incentives, hope is alive to reap heavily from lessons from the wasted past.

---

33 S.J. Stohle, Nigeria set to add LPG volumes to world trade, OH and Gas Journal, 2000; 98 (43): 54-61.
34 N. John Erinne, The Nigerian gas industry offers huge challenges and potentials, Oil and Gas Journal, 2001; 99 (76).

CHAPTER 16

Petroleum Technology Development Fund (PTDF)

The PTDF was established by a decree promulgated by the federal military government on 4 June 1973. The following funds were paid into the PTDF:
1. The balance of monetary assets outstanding in the accounts of the Gulf Oil Company Training Fund.
2. All further sums payable to, or received by the federal government, in terms of any agreement made by the government and any company in relation to petroleum prospecting or mining concessions.
3. Any other sums from time to time freely donated or accruing to the government or the fund for the training and education of Nigerians in the petroleum industry.

The Fund was to be available for the purposes of training Nigerians to qualify as graduates, professionals, technicians and craftsmen, in the fields of engineering, geology, science and management in the petroleum industry in Nigeria or abroad.[35]

The PTDF decree effectively repealed the Gulf Oil Company Training Fund (Administration) Act 1964. In order to ensure that the funds were properly utilized, The Public Funds of the Federation (Disbursement) Rules 1959 act was amended and enlarged and renamed Public Fund of the Federation (Disbursement *Amendment*) Rules, which commenced on 18 June 1973. The sixth schedule was amended to specify the following:
1. To provide scholarships and bursaries, wholly or partially, in universities, colleges, institutions and in petroleum undertakings in Nigeria and abroad;

---

[35] Petrol Technology Development Fund Decree No. 25, 1973. Federal Military! Government of Nigeria. Lagos, 4 June 1974.

2. To maintain, supplement or subsidize such training or education as mentioned above;
3. To make suitable endowment to faculties in Nigerian universities, colleges or institutions in Nigeria;
4. To make available suitable books and training equipment in the institution aforesaid;
5. To sponsor regular, or as necessary, visits to oilfields, refineries, petrochemical plants and for arranging any necessary attachments of personnel to establishments connected with the development of the petroleum industry;
6. To finance participation in seminars and conferences which are connected with the petroleum industry in Nigeria and abroad.

The fund was administratively put in the Department of Petroleum Resources [DPR) of the Ministry of Petroleum Resources [MPR). It was moved to the presidency in 2000, where it got a boost, in terms of inflow of funds and public awareness. However, political influence and abuse crept into the deployment of the PTDF.[36] The presidency quickly set up a new structure in the Office of the Vice President. An interim management committee was created in September 2000, and a substantive executive secretary/CEO was appointed.

Unfortunately, political interference suddenly emerged on the question of the appointment of the CEO, in a political power play among the power brokers in the ruling People's Democratic Party (PDP) in Kaduna. Added to the crisis was the misunderstanding between Obasanjo and his vice between 2005 and 2007, when the PTDF became a major political battle field among the powerful members of the ruling political party. Grave allegations were made openly in the press about gross diversion, misappropriation and theft. It is ironic that all alleged malpractices were related to expenditure outside the statutory functions of the PTDF.

---

36 Nigerian Muse. The Use and Abuse of the PTDF, 28 June 2009, (www.nigerianmuse.com/ 2009).

This crisis, which plagued the fund for several years, is characteristic of the history of the oil and gas sector in Nigeria. Over the years, the technical control of the sector was unaddressed by the government, because of the lack of will to take the bull by the horns and, clearly, the pervasive power of corruption. Since the end of the Obasanjo administration, which had a stranglehold on the institutions in the petroleum sector, the fund has embarked on activities to ensure that the objectives of the PTDF are pursued and realized. For instance, it was decided that a National Centre for Skills Development and Training in Oil and Gas be established in 2008. Additional centres were planned to follow. The PTDF set up the first oil and gas polytechnic in Ekowe, Bayelsa State, and admitted its first set of students in June 2012. Serious attention is now being paid to the award of scholarships and grants to universities to enhance their teaching and research.

CHAPTER 17
Nigerian Content Development

An important factor for consideration during the 2000, 2005 and 2006 bid rounds for oil blocks was whether a bidder could demonstrate a strong commitment to the development of Nigerian expertise as part of its intended operations. Specifically, the question was whether a bidder incorporated any local content. In order to make a successful bid, bidders were required to establish that they would use Nigerian goods and services in their operations. In the 2005 bid round, however, the requirement was modified for the bidder to link its bids with 'local content vehicles', in the form of locally incorporated companies, with a majority of Nigerian shareholders that would provide the goods and services required to execute their bids if they succeeded.

The idea of local content in the oil and gas sector is traceable to the Petroleum Act 1969 (as amended), the principal statute which regulates the oil and gas industry. The act requires that holders of oil mining leases ensure that 75 % of their supervisory, managerial and professional employees are Nigerian within ten years of the grant of leases. In addition, no less than 60 % of the employees in any of these grades must be Nigerian, while all semi-skilled and unskilled employees must be Nigerian.

In order to actualize the local content goal, the federal government has tried to entrench the scheme within the oil and gas sector by, among other things, taking the following steps:
1. Incorporation of specific provisions in joint operating agreements and production sharing contracts designed to encourage the employment of Nigerians.
2. The establishment of the Petroleum Training Institute and Petroleum Technology Fund to support the training of Nigerians for the petroleum industry.

3. The issuance of guidelines with respect to the release of Nigerian workers from employment in the Petroleum Industry and Utilization Quota in 1997, with a view to increasing Nigerian participation in the petroleum industry.
4. The development of the marginal field programme pursuant to the Petroleum Act and the Guidelines for Farm-out and Operation of Marginal Fields issued by the Department of Petroleum Resources in 2001 to encourage the participation of Nigerians in the petroleum industry.
5. The issuance of Nigerian Content-Development Short-Term Directives in 2006, which require that:
   - All project management teams and procurement centres for all projects in the sector should be relocated to Nigeria.
   - Nigerian companies should participate in all tenders.
   - Evidence of binding agreements with Nigerian subcontractors (detailing the goods and services to be procured in Nigeria) should be provided.
   - Front-end engineering and detailed engineering designs for all projects (including seismic data processing projects and reservoir management studies) should be carried out in Nigeria by the end of 2005.
   - The fabrication of certain categories of equipment (e.g. top sides of fixed onshore and offshore platforms weighing up to 5,000 tonnes, carbon steel pressure vessels of no more than 75 millimetres steel thickness, piles, decks anchors, buoys, jackets, bridges, flare booms and storage tanks) should be carried out in Nigeria.
   - Equipment and materials manufactured in Nigeria should be fully utilized.
   - Clauses that create impediments or exclude Nigerian companies from participation in any tender should be removed.
   - The establishment of a National Committee of Local Content Development in 2003 and the submission of The Nigerian Oil and Gas Industry Content Act to the National Assembly, on the basis of the national committee's report.

The passage of the Petroleum (Drilling and Production) Regulation, 1969, required holders of oil mining leases or oil prospecting licenses to submit to the minister of Petroleum Resources for approval, within twelve months of the grant of the licenses or leases, a detailed programme of the recruitment and training of Nigerians in all phases of petroleum operations, whether the phases are handled directly by the companies or through their agents.

The development was heavily criticized, but the act was passed, which established an integrated legal and operational framework for the development of local content in the oil and gas industry. The act adds flesh to existing laws on the matter and specifically defines 'Nigerian Content' thus:

'... the quantum of composite value added to or created in the Nigerian economy through a deliberate utilization of Nigerian human and material resources and services in the upstream sector of the Nigerian petroleum industry, which includes all activities connected with the exploration, development, exploitation, transportation and sale of Nigerian crude oil and gas resources, without compromising quality, health safety and environmental standards'.

The Nigerian Oil and Gas Industry Content Act, 2003 additionally seeks to implement the intention to ensure full compliance with its local content policy. The bill empowers the Department of Petroleum Resources, the regulator of the Nigerian oil and gas industry, to monitor the performance of all its joint operation partners, contractors and service providers, with a view to bringing their activities into conformity with the provisions of the bill, which aims at achieving 45 % local content in 2006 and 70 % by 2010.

The Nigerian Oil and Gas Industry Content Development Act was signed into law on April 22, 2010, to apply to all operators in the Nigerian oil and gas sector, including exploration, production and service companies. Two major provisions point to the aim of the act:

1. Section 3 (1): Nigerian independent operators shall be given first consideration in the award of oil blocks, oil field licenses, oil lifting licenses and all projects for which contracts will be awarded.
2. Section 3 (2): Exclusive consideration to be given to Nigerian indigenous service companies, which demonstrate ownership of equipment, Nigerian personnel and capacity to execute work on land and swamp operating areas.[37]

The new oil and gas industry content development comes as a cumulative outcome of several years of attempts by the government and stakeholders in the petroleum industry to ensure the provision of local value-added to Nigeria. The awareness, after fifty years of oil exploration and Nigeria's attainment of independence, broke the myth of Nigeria being regarded as an enclave economy, offering little connection to the broader economy. The act offers great opportunities for growth and expansion to indigenous operators in the sector and tremendous benefits to indigenous service companies.

Aderemi Ogunbanjo presents an exhaustive overview of the content development act in one of his papers on the subject.[38] The objective of the act is to transform the oil and gas sector into an economic engine for job creation and national development by domestic capacity-building in manpower and technology. All the principles of the directives have been provided for in the proposed Petroleum Industry Bill.

Prior to the emergence of the Nigerian Content Act, the Erha Development Project, the first to prescribe a minimum Nigerian content, included the award of contracts and subcontracts to several Nigerian companies to provide in-country fabrication,

---

37 Dayo Okusami, An Overview of the Nigerian Local Content Act, Africa Energy Week Conference, Cape Town, 29 September 2010.
38 Aderemi Ogunbanjo. An Overview of the Nigerian Oil and Gas Industry Content Development Act 2010, 2010 (www.scribd.com/doc/30564109) (Accessed on 29 April 2010).

logistic support, training and recruitment of Nigerians. After the enactment of the act, giant steps have continued to be taken by oil companies in keeping with the objectives of the act. The Erha Development Project demonstrates ExxonMobil's commitment to the achievement of Nigerian content in oil and gas operations. The project created the first Subsea Systems Integration Test (SIT) in Nigeria and was achieved at the Willbros facility in Port Harcourt, which now acts as a regional centre for subsequent SIT activities. ExxonMobil holds a 56 % interest in the Erha project situated on OPL 209. Progress is being made in the implementation of the provisions of the act, as seen in the reduction in the reliance of oil companies on foreign logistics and services.

It is worth repeating, what was mentioned in the second paragraph of this chapter – that the concept of local content is not new to Nigeria. Okusami[39] noted in 2010, that the Petroleum Act of 1969 provided for local content in its schedule, which required the holder of an oil mining lease (OML) ensure that 75 % of managerial, professional and supervisory staff should be Nigerians within ten years from the grant of the lease. Furthermore, production sharing contracts (PSC) and joint operating agreements (JOA) also contained local content provisions.

---

[39] Dayo Okusami, Local Content Law – Is this the one, All Africa, 25 May 2010

CHAPTER 18
The Reform Agenda

It became obvious that the legal and management structures which were designed over five decades ago are no longer capable of catering for the requirements of today's oil and gas industry. For instance, several acts enacted and amended since the early seventies are contained in several instruments dispersed in several documents, making it difficult to make easy reference to them. Similarly, all the institutions governing the sector were essentially civil service departments, which were not equipped to conceive policy choices and formulations necessary for a complex industry. The greatest problem is the capacity of the NNPC, a huge cost-centre too amorphous to lead the industry effectively. Thus, after decades of trial and error, with dependence on the international oil companies, Nigeria woke up to the reality of the weaknesses in the governance of her oil and gas industry.

The draft Petroleum Industry Bill (PIB) produced by the Reform Implementation Committee turned out to be much more than an exercise to transform policy into law.[40] It became clear that it was necessary to take into consideration several overriding issues so as to create a law that will fully encapsulate the legal and governance requirements of a complex industry.

As a result, the committee sought for and obtained submissions from various public institutions inside and outside the industry. It also received submissions from key stakeholders, including the oil producing trade sector of the chamber of commerce and key downstream operators. The draft bill is a detailed document covering most of the issues pertaining to oil and gas exploration,

---

40 E.O. Egbogah. Oil and Gas Sector Reforms in Nigeria: What you should know, www.dreghogah.com/documents/69.html.

production, transportation and marketing. Other matters covered include state participation and control, fiscal issues, regulation, safety, health, environmental concerns and community relations.

Egbogah[41], Omose[42] Legal[43] and Sahara Reporters[44] dwelt on the subject exhaustively in separate reports and papers published on the subject at different times. Obviously, the proposed bill poses a serious challenge to the international oil companies (IOCs) and some strong interests in the NNPC. A showdown emerged in the discussion between government and the IOCs, who foresaw a nationalistic posture, higher royalties, tax and reduced equity participation. The campaign by oil companies to change the terms in the bill gathered momentum. At a point, Shell's vice-president of exploration and production for Africa, Ann Pickard[45] said that the bill would make Nigeria's production sharing contracts (PSC) "among the harshest in the world", and "all or almost all proposed desperate projects will become uneconomic."

ExxonMobil also joined the fray, when they stated that they were unanimous that deep-water development was threatened by the terms of the bill. Total also joined by voicing a conciliatory note publicly, hoping for a mutually agreeable outcome in the discussions.

In a Wikileaks document on Nigeria, posted on 24 January 2011, by Sahara Reporters, New York, very grave revelations were contained in several exchanges between Shell Exec-

---

41 Ibid.
42 Kingsley Amose, Nigeria, Wikileaks and Moles in High Places, (eliesmith. blogspot.com 2010, 11 December 2010, and (elombah.com. www.elombah. com/index)
43 Debbie Legall. New Petroleum Industry Bill for Nigeria. International Bar Association, UK.
44 Sahara Reporters. Wikileaks On Nigeria: Shell's Ann Pickard Says Tural, Tanimu and NNPC GMD Yar'adua Were Collecting Bribes from Oil Lifting Contracts, 24 January 2011.
45 IHS Global Insight Oil Majors Pick Up Campaign to Modify Nigeria's Petroleum Industry Bill, 3 November 2010.

utive, Ann Pickard, and the US Ambassador, which portray the extent of Shell's involvement in the political schemes in Nigeria and, particularly, in the campaign against the Petroleum Industry Reform Bill. Some of the exchanges are very damning and extremely damaging, showing how far foreign interests may go to undermine Nigeria's strategic policy plans to protect their own economic interests. With trillions of cubic feet of proven natural gas reserves, over thirty billion barrels of proven oil reserves and an exponential deep-water production growth, Nigeria is faced with the challenge of how to manage her enormous mineral prospects.

Domestic discontent with the status quo, an unending fuel scarcity, inability to sustain uninterrupted electricity supply and the breakdown of the refineries have drawn attention to the urgent need to bring radical reforms to the governance of the sector.

The Petroleum Industry Bill was introduced in the senate in January 2009, aiming to start on a clean slate by repealing all existing legislative instruments relating to the oil and gas sector, including the Petroleum Profit Tax. It contains some 496 clauses to transform the industry, now largely dominated by the Nigerian National Petroleum Corporation (NNPC), which the government is convinced has failed to drive the sector effectively.[46] What is captured in the bill with regard to structure and interaction is a new industry with a vision to perform creditably.

The PIB Committee believe that the implementation of the proposed reforms will open up the Nigerian oil and gas sector to new local and international investors for competitive growth and sustainable development by:
1. Creating a modern petroleum legal framework.
2. Aligning the Nigerian oil and gas sector to international best practices.
3. Enhancing transparency and an open framework.

---

46 The National and Gas Policy, (www.nigerianalitesforum.com/ng reports and issues/2337).

4. Establishing good governance practices and processes.
5. Reinforcing linkages between the oil and gas industry and other sectors of the Nigerian economy.
6. Supporting the energy objectives of government.[47]

NNPC's position is very firm, dismissing any suggesting that the bill would have an adverse effect on the industry. In a reaction to arguments advanced by the international oil companies against the bill, the NNPC dismissed their position that the proposed bill would make Nigeria's production sharing contracts (PSC), which stand at 42 %, the harshest in the world, with an average of 75 %. It stated that it is 78 % in Angola, 76 % in Norway and Ghana is proposing 80 %.

The NNPC added that the liquefied natural gas (NLG) plant in Bonny was operated for ten years by the international oil companies without paying any tax at all because of a tax holiday which was meant to encourage investment. They also added that Nigeria now knows that 80 % of every dollar invested in the industry goes offshore through objectionable recruitment of low level foreign staff, like cooks and stewards by the international oil companies, but that the practice will no longer be allowed.

The controversy which the PIB engenders reflects both anger and diplomacy on both sides of the argument. The strength of the argument in defence of the bill by Nigerian stakeholders, particularly the indigenous operators and local service companies, portrays the chequered journey of the Nigerian oil and gas sector since oil was struck in Oloibiri.

The bill seeks to break up the NNPC into seven distinct companies and create a National Petroleum Company of Nigeria (NAPCON) as a private commercial company. The new company will inherit NNPC's shares in existing joint ventures with Shell, ExxonMobil, Chevron, Total and Eni and, eventu-

---

47 An Overview of the Petroleum Industry Bill, July 2009 (www.nnpcgroup.com/Portals/0/pdf/PIBConsultativeForum.pdf).

ally, incorporate joint ventures as independent entities able to conduct business with funds directly sourced from the financial market. The troubling aspect of the bill concerns the review of existing concessions and contracts which the government considers to favour the international oil companies, most of which were signed several years ago. The bill does not seek to terminate existing agreements, but a review.

The downstream sector will be deregulated to remove the burden on the government of having to pay heavily to subsidize fuel importation for domestic consumption, a situation which makes it hard for the government to invest adequately in the upkeep of existing refineries and the construction of new ones.

The reforms emphasize local participation in the sector, by way of using local content as an important condition for the award of oil licences for oil exploration, to ensure the promotion, at all times, of the use of indigenous companies, employees and locally-produced goods and services. The bill has not yet passed due to delays and political confrontations with powerful interest groups opposed to the reforms.

Whatever happens, the need for reforms seems to be compelling so that Nigerians may reap from her rich oil and gas resources. The thrust of the proposed reforms is the transformation of the Nigerian National Petroleum Corporation, from a position of guardian of government's interests, into an integrated, international commercial corporation by splitting it up.

In his analysis of the proposed restructuring, Joe Brock[48] insists that plans to overhaul Nigeria's oil and gas sector through the Petroleum Industry Bill (PIB) will not make Nigeria less attractive to investors than her peers in the industry, but the overhaul will not immediately provide answers to the problem of funding, security and corruption which plague the industry. The

---

48 Joe Brock. Analysis – Nigeria Still to Be Competitive After Oil Reforms. Reuters, 11 March 2011.

PIB is designed to impose royalties and increase taxes on profitable offshore projects, but experts insist that funding and security are the real obstacles to the health of the Nigerian oil and gas industry. In April 2010, PIB was withdrawn by the government for review to accommodate the position of the international oil corporations. The reviewed version of the bill was returned to the National Assembly in July 2012. About 14 years since the idea of the bill was initiated, the proposal has not matured into legislation. Each time it moves to become a law, what Nigerians are told is that the PIB will become legislation soon. Somehow, our SOON has not materialized. The story of the Petroleum Industry Bill is symptomatic of the Nigerian dilemma whose axis revolves round corruption. The debates over the PIB have now moved into 2014.

Contrary to the claims by the oil companies, the main obstacles to the reform and for the country are not in the formal fiscal terms, which experts believe have been generous compared to the other OPEC members. The main obstacles have been funding the joint ventures and the frustration in working with partners who are unable to provide funding. Security and corruption only compound the problem.

Moreover, it appears that the reservations expressed by the international oil companies are not well grounded, as could be seen already, the proposed new offshore terms would put Nigeria's terms at par with Angola, Brazil and Indonesia. It will be difficult for the oil companies to contradict Nigeria on this fact. The bill finally made it to the presidency on June 2012, from where it is expected to go to the national assembly.

CHAPTER 19
The Cost of Sabotage

The oil and gas resources in the Niger Delta have brought more misery than joy to the region because of the failure of governance. Despite the massive earnings from oil and gas since 1958, the Niger Delta remains in abject poverty and dire need of attention. The World Bank estimates that about 90 % of the Niger Delta people are poor.[49] The Niger Delta is the home of Nigeria's wealth and about 90 % of her foreign exchange. For several decades, disaffection has brewed slowly, but noticeably, among the people of the oil region. Somehow, the signs have been consistently ignored, while the political class lived in opulence and open abuse of power. It was therefore not surprising when the sabotage of oil production reared its head.

While the politicians and higher echelons of the military have found great riches at the expense of the treasury, the people's health and sources of earnings were destroyed by years of oil spills, and gas flaring, with the region becoming one of the most polluted places in the world. The pain which brought the deepened grievances obviously became too much for the people of the region. The result was the expression of their disaffection through militancy. The consequences are in the forms of bunkering, kidnaping, destruction of pipelines and killing of oil workers. The political elite looked the other way as the atrocities escalated, because much of the bunkering operations can be linked to them. It may be suggested that material deprivation provided the inspiration for the Niger Delta anger, so to say, but it is realistic also to accept that the dysfunctional political dynamics are the undergirding factors that inflamed and promot-

---

49 Nigeria Oil and Gas Report, Quarter 2, pp. 68–72, 2011.

ed the incipient grievances into the violence, which became difficult to quell by force.

Kew and Phillips[50] explored the Niger Delta story exhaustively in their study published in 2006, in which they took a deep look at the political background of the Niger Delta region, which provides a much wider insight. The crisis is a grave threat to the Nigerian oil and gas operations and export. The amnesty seems to have provided a relief for now, but will the amnesty strategy sustain a permanent peace? It is not possible to predict.

By the year 2008, Nigeria was at risk of losing its reliability as a supplier of crude oil because of worsening attacks which held back exports. It was that anxiety over the disruptions that helped to push oil forecasts to about $90 a barrel. Nigeria was producing less than 2.2 million barrels of oil per day as at December 2008, although it had a production capacity of about 3 million barrels then.[51] That meant that over half a million barrels were lost in production daily. It affected the oil companies and the nation, with a consequent failure to meet export market commitments. Apart from production shutdown in some cases, development projects were halted, suspended or simply abandoned by the oil companies. These steps have had far reaching consequences for the industry.

A major cause of the uncertainty in the oil producing region is the decision by Shell to sell some of its stakes in a member of licences. Shell, the pioneer oil major in Nigeria, was reconsidering its future commitments in Nigeria in consequence of the sabotage which has led to the loss of lives and oil production over the years. It said that, although Nigeria remains a heartland for the company, it no longer depends on the country for its growth ambition. Also, it was of the opinion that there is a lot to devel-

---

50 Daren Kew and D.L. Phillips. Seeking peace in the Niger Delta: Oil, natural gas and other vital resources. New England Journal of Public Policy 2006; 21 (2): 154–170.
51 A. Henshall. Nigeria's oil-export reliability at risk, Wall Street journal, 2008; 414.

op, but the Nigerian circumstances are not right.[52] Nigeria thus was not of high priority for Shell's future investment plans. What may be seen as a loss to the oil major, Shell, may as well be an advantage for new investors though.

Crude exports were below capacity for a period in the wake of the disruptions caused by militants in the oil producing region. The militants wanted a greater share of oil revenue for their communities ravaged by poverty, environmental damage to their farmlands and the pollution of their waterways. Poverty in the Niger Delta is ubiquitous, despite the wealth accruing to Nigeria from their land. As a result of the sabotage to the oil installations, threats to the staff of oil companies and loss of earnings, the federal government offered amnesty to the militants in August 2009, when an unsuccessful military operation did not deter them. Government engaged in reconciliation with the disaffected communities who felt justifiably abandoned by government and left at the mercy of the oil companies, whom they consider as their adversaries, who reap heavily from their land at their expense.

The amnesty initiative involved a monthly payment of a certain amount to the militants in exchange for ending their disruptive assaults on oil installations and the murder of oil staff. It was clearly appreciated by government that MEND possessed a good knowledge of the geography of the riverine territory that constitutes the Niger Delta. That knowledge was to their advantage, resulting in the failure of a military approach to weaken their effective sabotage.

Amnesty was announced on 24 June 2009, with centres set up in six southern states to receive arms surrendered by the militants, after voluntarily taking an oath to abandon their militancy, for which an unconditional pardon was given.

Government then hoped that the initiative would pave the way for the realization of an end to the violence in the region,

---

52 Will Shell pull out of Nigeria? African Business, 2010, pp.

but observers were understandably sceptical about the outcome. There were justifiable reservations that the scheme could not address the long-term problem, but contrary to the reservations, the programme appears to have succeeded so far. There still remains some scepticism because of the nature of the division among the various fighting groups and the corruption among the administrators of the scheme. But the government hopes that the oil production increases resulting from the absence or reduction of sabotage would make up for the cost of the scheme.

MEND's reaction to the amnesty was initially doubtful because of the nature of the organization, which boasts of having a number of groups but no central authority. While some of MEND's leaders accepted the amnesty and participated in it, others were half-hearted about it, with some rejecting it outright.

MEND nevertheless announced a ceasefire in July 2009, for two months, providing time for negotiations. In August 2009, a public ceremony was held with fanfare, at which hundreds of militants handed over their weapons and gunboats. After the public ceremony in Yenagoa, Bayelsa State, one of the leaders of MEND, Jomo Gbomo, denounced the exercise as fake and stage-managed by the government. MEND condemned the financial incentives given to militants and warned that the only solution to the crisis was a process whereby, the real roots of the unrest were fully addressed. MEND called off talks with the presidency and the state governors. Jomo Gbomo declared that MEND would resume attacks on oil facilities by 15 September 2009.

That threat was aborted and MEND chose to continue negotiations with the government. A team called *Aaron* was selected by MEND on 29 September 2009, comprising Okhai Akhigbe, Luke Aprezi, Wole Soyinka and Sabella Abidde to address the causes of the unrest. After a meeting between Henry Okah and Umaru Yar'Adua on 19 October 2009, MEND announced a ceasefire starting from 25 October 2009.

By early 2010, MEND dramatically called off the ceasefire that was declared in October 2009. Jomo Gbomo declared a full onslaught against installations and personnel of oil companies operating in the Niger Delta. The announcement of the end of MEND's ceasefire was followed by reports that Shell had shut down three oil flow stations after the Trans Ramos pipeline in Bayelsa was sabotaged.

In spite of the amnesty in place, the fundamental causes of the violence in the Niger Delta remained, particularly the degradation of the environment and the glaring neglect of the region. In March 2010, a little-known militant group, called the Joint Revolutionary Council (JRC), announced a blow up of the Abbiama Oil manifold in Buguma and promised to reduce the exports to zero with an increased intensity of attacks. It had announced before, in February, that it had blown up Shell's Tura manifold which links to the Bonny export terminal. It also said that a pipeline in Chanomi Creek carrying crude oil to the Kaduna refinery had been attacked. These renewed attacks resulted in a reduction in oil production. For instance, after attacks on its Forcados Stream Pipeline, which caused a drop in production from 175,000 barrels per day in the fourth quarter by 2009, to 25,000 barrels per day, Shell said it was considering the sale of some of their assets.

This crisis has endured for decades without Nigeria being able to arrest it. The problem remains partially obscured by the amnesty, which observers view with doubt. For a very long time, the most effective way to get the attention of oil companies was to cause violence. Thus, the best security is to ensure that the communities' welcome and hospitality, which are not available free of charge.

The juxtaposition of extreme poverty and wealth does not make for happy bedfellows. Successive Nigerian governments have mishandled and often ignored the affected populations in the Niger Delta-and then turn around and blamed the oil companies. The military regimes ran rough shod over the communities in the Delta, driving out any opposition to the oil companies.

Local communities have learnt that they are more likely to get a share of the benefits of oil if they are bold enough to invade an oil rig, seize a company's helicopter or take a staff hostage. Able-bodied men who seek jobs by threatening the companies with cutlasses and wooden clubs are sometimes put on the payroll, draw such wages, but do not have to report for work. In that way, the companies are happy. This kind of payment is a form of protection fee, which is part of the cost of doing business in the region. Guest[53] said this much when he insisted that oil alone does not make Nigeria happy.

What has happened to the industry in recent years is a sobering fact, but even the use of amnesty to quell the attacks by angry militants is an undependable solution as long as oil industry players and the Nigerian political culture remain deep in corruption and poor governance. It is impossible to calculate the actual cost of sabotage, but it is clear that it is enormous.

---

53 R. Guest Nigeria. Oil alone doesn't make you happy. The Economist, 2000, pp. 8–10.

CHAPTER 20
Environmental Consequences

Nigeria's Niger Delta region, home of the oil wealth that provides a greater part of the revenue which funds the massive Nigerian government, is largely undeveloped and polluted with oil spoils which have been left to fester for decades depriving these poor riverine people of a means of livelihood. Nobody can say how much oil has gone into the rivers and creeks, but observers and environmental campaigners say that the ecological impact is one of the worst in the world.

Oil companies claim that spills are caused by militant attacks or sabotage. Royal Dutch Shell says it cleans up oil spills as quickly as possible, no matter what the causes are, but says that delays occur because of obstruction from communities or security problems. Some fishermen cannot continue with their fishing because pollution has destroyed the waters, killing off the fish and other natural resources. Most farmers thus have no choice but to take to crude oil theft to make a living. Shell is said to have lost about 100,000 barrels of crude oil to spills in 2009 alone, largely due to attacks on pipelines.

The United Nations Environment Programme (UNEP) team investigating oil spills in the Niger Delta region, over several decades, has provided a very bleak picture of groundwater contamination and major damage to the mangrove swamps. The report attributed part of the problem to sabotage by local groups engaged in stealing oil. By their assessment, the team suggested that only 10 % of leaks were caused by carelessness on the part of the oil companies, while 90 % were from oil theft and the militant activities.[54] The communities and human rights groups dis-

---

54 Exploration and production Blame row threatens Niger Delta clean-up. UN Environment Programme (UNEP). Petroleum Economist (0306 396) 2010.

agree with the argument, saying, while oil theft rose sharply in recent years, most of the pollution since oil exploration started in the region has been caused by the oil companies. Shell is singled out as the major culprit. But the company denies this assertion, saying that actions by armed militants and oil theft by local gangs have contributed largely to oil spillage. Shell says that nearly 100,000 barrels of crude oil were spilled into the marshes and creeks in 2009.

The Niger Delta has witnessed conflicts between the government forces and the local militants, who claim they are fighting for access to the fortunes coming from their own land. While the argument rages about the cost of exploration and the parties to hold responsible, the UNEP team has rejected the figures being touted by the oil major, saying that, as a matter of fact, its one-year study in the Ogoni region was not even completed yet, not to talk of its publication at the time. The statement from UNEP[55] was used as ammunition for those who feel that the oil companies were about to steamroll the situation to be absolved from blame.

The reasonable thing to do is to take a very dispassionate look at the problems of environmental degradation in the region, with the concerted efforts of all the stakeholders in solving the problems.

Another cause of the environmental degradation of the Niger Delta is the menace of gas flaring, which may well have contributed more to the greenhouse gas level of the atmosphere. Campaigners say that gas flaring causes acid rain and pollutes groundwater. Life expectancy has fallen over the years in the oil producing region as a result of the systematic reduction in the quality of life of the inhabitants of the communities. The scenario has become more aggravated, recently, with the announcement that the Ogale people in Eleme Community are suing Shell in a US court, to seek recompense to the tune of $1 billion, for the damage inflicted on them over five decades years of pollution. The

---

55 Ibid.

people are accusing Shell of gross negligence and deliberate degradation by the company during over fifty years of oil exploration and gas flaring. This development points to the misfortune which characterizes the derivation of enormous revenue through the activities of oil companies in the Niger Delta area of Nigeria.

Ugochukwu and Ertel in their exhaustive work on the negative impacts of oil exploration stated that the burying of oil and gas pipelines in the Niger Delta fragments rich ecosystems such as the rainforests and the mangrove swamps.[56] Apart from the reduction in habitat area, the clearing of pipelines track segregates the natural populations.

They reported that there were 5,334 reported cases of crude oil spillages, which released about 2.8 million barrels of oil into the land, swamp, estuaries and coastal waters of Nigeria. The overall effects of these oil spillages on the health of the ecosystem are multidimensional. For instance, leakages and fire occurrences are also associated with gas production, flaring and transportation. Whenever there is a fire accident, the fire burns endlessly, killing plants and animals, thereby eliminating whole populations of endangered species.

---

56 C.N.C. Ugochukwu and J. Ertel, Negative impacts of oil exploration in biodiversity management in the Niger Delta area of Nigeria. Impact Assessment and Project Appraisal, 2008; 26 (2): 139–147.

CHAPTER 21
Triumph of Failure

On 22 November 2011, the governor of the Central Bank of Nigeria was reported to have said that Nigeria must renegotiate offshore oil contracts. He told an audience in Abuja that the fiscal terms of present contracts are unfavourable to the country.[57] Oil companies should renegotiate or get out, he said. Deep-water operations account for 40 % of Nigeria's oil production, with about $5 billion loss to Nigeria in a year, contributing to the decline of the country's foreign reserves. As usual, the grave allegation by the CBN head ought to translate into serious action on the part of those who are in charge of the oil industry.

The government of the day has been openly challenged by Nigerians to confront the cartel, which has made progress impossible in the industry, particularly in the sphere of oil refining. One politician alleged recently that the metres for reading the quantity of crude oil exported by Nigeria have not yet been fixed. It was alleged that the NNPC officials are not interested in fixing the metres, so as to hide the amount of crude oil being lifted. Most people are of the opinion that the four refineries do not receive the amount of crude oil allocated to them daily, because the NNPC officials prefer to sell the allocation. A probe by the Senate Committee revealed a portion of the 445,000 barrels allocated to the NNPC daily could not be unaccounted for. About two weeks after Shell shut down the 200,000 barrels per day, Bonga facility, the company announced the closure of operation of the Nembe Creek Trunkline. Some 70,000 barrels per day were thus shut-in because of crude theft leaks in the pipeline.

---

57 Nigeria must renegotiate offshore oil contracts, says Sanusi, The Nation, 22 November 2011.

Investigations showed that oil thieves installed valves at two points near the Tora manifold in Nembe. The Nembe Creek Trunkline was constructed at a cost of about $1.1 billion, with a capacity to transport 600,000 barrels per day from fourteen flow stations to the Bonny export terminal in Rivers State. The line had been attacked many times in the past. This shows that the deliberate attack by militants is one problem, while theft is another entirely. Shell said that the oil spill from the Bonga field is the largest spill in Nigeria since 1998. The spill was contained at great cost, but the oil field has been closed since the spill.

There is a peculiar paradox to Nigeria's enormous oil wealth, including the inestimable reserves of gas. Petroleum has brought more troubles to the country than any other factor. It has created huge political divisions and rivalries, it has supported runaway corruption and it has planted the seed of violence in the oil-producing region. This problem is the result of general incompetence at the NNPC and bad leadership in the federal government of Nigeria. From any oil-producing country's perspective, a competent national oil company with good governance is preferable to a privatization of the oil and gas industry. National oil companies should be able to respond to the needs of their societies and pursue national interests with dutiful commitment. With good financial management, they ought to generate more income for the state and protect such revenue. National oil companies from several countries such as China and Malaysia are conspicuous in the international arena, signing agreements and lucrative contracts in Saudi Arabia and Iran. Some national oil companies are creating privatized arms to engage in competitive exploits overseas. For instance, in a dramatic move in 2005, China's National Offshore Oil Corporation (CNOOC) bid to buy Western International Oil Company and UNOCAL. Russia also appears to be reasserting the role of the state in the oil and gas sector, when it dismantled the most successful private Russian company, Yukos Oil Company. This example shows the absurdity of the Nigerian situation, where the NNPC is performing so poorly, that there are strident calls for its scrapping.

The proposed Petroleum Industry Bill seeks to fragment the NNPC into independent, business-oriented organizations, able to compete in the local and international scenes. That goal is almost impracticable, because the Nigerian environment is unique and, perhaps strange, as a result of widespread corruption. Otherwise, why is it that, after more than five decades, the oil and gas industry has not helped to change the face of the nation.

Nigeria has earned enormously from oil, exporting about 2 million barrels of crude oil per day, at about $85 per barrel.[58] We can justifiably argue that enough has been earned from oil to transform the country from its present state of neglect. Nigerian roads are bad, the hospitals are poorly equipped and the educational institutions are in a poor state, with dilapidated and derelict school buildings. The railway system flopped several years ago and the Nigerian Airways collapsed. The only evidence of the fortune which came from oil is the wealth displayed by the super-rich men and women who find their way into the political platform. So where did the oil future go?

Somebody asked rhetorically, 'Nigerian oil, a blessing or a curse'? From the point of view of corruption and the sheer degradation of the Niger Delta environment, and the conflict which petroleum has brought on Nigerians, it is easy to accept that it has been more of a curse than a blessing. It is clear that Nigerians are generally endowed with forbearance, even in the face of uncommon difficulties caused by bad governance. The triumph of failure in Nigeria's development efforts is a classical paradox, too complex to diagnose easily.

On 1 January 2012, the much-chorused subsidy removal was enforced. Consequently, the pump price of petroleum was increased from N65.00 to N141.00 a litre.

The public outrage was unprecedented and spontaneous. Labour called a strike, which started on 9 January 2012. The pub-

---

58 In September and October 2013 the price per barrel was $112.00–113.00 see www.cenbank.org/rates/crudeoil.asp?year=2013.

lic rose with anger and protests throughout the country called 'Occupy Nigeria'. All businesses, shops, banks, hospitals and airports were closed. Those who did not join in the street protests stayed indoors and the streets were virtually empty.

What happened in the second week of the first month of 2012 captures eloquently the ugly picture of the Nigerian problem and, specifically, the ugly face of the oil and gas sector. The federal government claimed that more than N1 trillion was spent on the petroleum subsidy in 2011. They said that the amount was paid to suppliers of petroleum who were engaged to import petroleum.

Nigerians cried foul. Why did Nigeria have to import fuel for domestic consumption? After five decades of a harvest of fortunes from oil and gas, Nigeria's oil and gas industry's grave afflictions remain inefficiency and corruption. Of all the oil-producing countries in the world, the Nigerian case is a classic case of irony which defies analysis. With the righteous indignation displayed by the public during the week of the subsidy crisis, it is clear that the stage of incubation has been arrived at. The strike was called off on 16 January 2012, when damage had been done to the credibility of the government and the NNPC. To assume that the trouble is over is to court disaster. If the reduction of the pump price was done to assuage Nigerians, it is a very thin hope to conclude that the trouble is over.

Another evidence that the Nigerian oil sector is drowning in corruption has been brought to the open with a petition from the Liberian government, claiming that the NNPC supplied one million barrels of crude in excess of their order in 2009. This petition was tendered by a member of the House of Representatives ad hoc committee on the subsidy scheme, which has blown off the lid on the deep-seated corruption in the regime. The story says that the Liberian government ordered 10,000 barrels of crude; the NNPC allegedly used a Nigerian company to supply one million barrels in excess of the order. Unbelievably, the NNPC collected full payment for the excess supply but failed to remit the money to the federal government. At the end of January 2012, the governor of the Central Bank of Nigeria told the ad hoc committee that despite the actual payment of N1.736 trillion for subsidy on petroleum between January and December 2011, the CBN still had to honour outstanding payments.

The minister of petroleum was reported to have claimed that Nigeria consumed 35 million litres per day, which was the basis of the subsidy cost, but the executive secretary of the Petroleum Products Pricing Regulatory Agency (PPPRA) said the country consumed 59 million litres of petroleum per day, showing a difference of 24 million litres between figures submitted by both. The minister stoutly denied the PPPRA figure, saying that 35 million litres of petroleum were consumed daily. She denied ever saying that the payments for subsidy were based on 35 million litres. This argument between both representatives of important agencies tells much about the failure of leadership in the oil and gas sector.

When startling revelations started to emerge from the ad hoc committee, a Nigerian daily newspaper, *The Nation*, published a factsheet on pages 2 and 3 of its 6 February 2012 edition, which tells the story of the management of the infamous subsidy regime. In 2011, the sum of N245 billion was budgeted for subsidy payment, but N1.348 trillion was said to have been paid to the petroleum importers. A staggering sum of $196 million was paid in two years as demurrage by the NNPC, while oil tankers waited to be offloaded at the ports.

Records showed that 35 million litres of oil was consumed daily in the country, but importers were paid for 59 million litres daily, giving a difference of 24 million litres, which was paid for fraudulently. This fraud has gone unchecked for a long time, but no one in government is ready to take responsibility for the practice.

The minister of finance denied ever giving the NNPC any authority to deduct subsidy payments before remitting funds to the Federation Account. It was revealed that the ministry of finance in conjunction with the PPPRA has been paying billions of naira as subsidy for fuel not consumed by Nigerians since 2006.

CHAPTER 22
As If There is No Future …

The story of the oil and gas industry in Nigeria is a history of leadership failure, political greed and moral bankruptcy on a grand scale. One wonders if there is another country where their oil sector has been so shamelessly abused in the same way Nigeria has misused hers. What has been revealed since January 2012, as a result of the removal of the oil subsidy, has come as a rude shock to many. The behaviour of the Nigerian public officers, the civil service and the political group is a huge shame. This chapter is a turning point in the chronicle of the history of the Nigerian oil and gas sector. Some newspaper articles and commentaries have been elected to provide a window into the ugliness of the practices throughout the sector.

In Nigeria, senior civil servants steal pension funds, another member of the ruling party joins the fuel theft gang and a top officer of the NNPC engages in bunkering. An account was opened secretly for the proceeds of crude oil by the federal government, but NNPC says it has no hand in the operation of the account. The minister of finance does not have details of the account and all finders are pointing to the CBN, which was said to be the signatory to the account. It is not clear why those who are entrusted with power and its deployment in Nigeria are so notoriously predisposed to corrupt practices. The newspaper articles assembled in this chapter will make you either laugh at or weep for Nigeria.

1. Nigeria's Oil Minister Inaugurates Petroleum Revenue Special Task Force. BBC Monitoring Africa, 29 February 2012.

Malam Nuhu Ribadu promised a tough regime for unscrupulous players in Nigeria's oil sector. He was speaking after the inauguration of the Petroleum Revenue Special Task Force by the minister of petroleum resources, Diezani Allison-Madueke. The 21-member task force was set up by the federal government to enhance probity and accountability in the operation of Nigeria's oil industry. Ribadu declared that the game was finally over. He stressed that the existing operational modalities in the oil sector was opaque and there was thus the need to enthrone acceptable moral standards. He said that most Nigerians do not think highly of the conduct of the oil and gas operations. 'The moral terrain of the industry has always been defined by the kind of value and concept of resource curse', he declared.

The task force is to work with consultants to determine and verify all petroleum upstream and downstream revenues, take all necessary steps to collect all debts, and obtain agreements and enforce payment terms by all industry operators. They were expected to complete their task within two months, subject to extension.

2. Subsidy Report: We've been Vindicated, says NEITI.
This Day, 7 May 2012

The Nigerian Extractive Industries Transparency Initiative (NEITI) said that the report of the House of Representative ad hoc committee on administration of petroleum subsidy has finally validated the value of its audit findings on the petroleum sector. According to NEITI, the report of the probe panel, which indicted the NNPC, PPPRA, CBN and some other stakeholders in the sector, was comprehensive. NEITI also said that it was not surprised by the findings and that it had earlier, in an audit report, made some damning revelations of underhand practices in the oil sector. NEITI has variously accused NNCP and others of short changing the federation of un-remitted revenue from crude sales. For NEITI, the probe report by the house confirmed the prevailing poor institutional linkages, infrastructural weakness, governance and process lapses, as well as some form of impurity which appeared to frustrate efforts at enthroning openness, transparency and good business ethics in the oil and gas industry over the years.

3. Fuel Subsidy Probe: Who Pulls the Strings? The Nation: 8 May 2012

Victor Oluwasegun and Dele Anofi wrote in an article that there was no doubt that the eight-member House of Representatives ad hoc committee on fuel subsidy management stirred up a hornet's nest. The report catalogued monumental infractions in the management of the subsidy funds. The reports called for the refund of N1.07 trillion by the Nigerian National Petroleum Corporation (NNPC), Petroleum Products Pricing Regulatory Authority (PPPRA) and several oil marketers. The report wants NNPC to refund N595.49 billion to the Federation Account, and the trial of the executive secretary of the PPPRA who served between 2009 and 2011. The report pointed out that Nigeria spent N2.587 trillion on fuel subsidy up to 31 December 2011, rather than the conflicting official figures of N1.3 trillion, N1.6 trillion and N1.7 trillion from the PPPRA, OAGF and CBN. The report initially blamed the former accountant general of the federation for the payment of N999 million 128 times on 12 and 13 January 2009. The report recommended a total reorganization of NNPC.

4. Jonathan Unwilling to Risk Oil Graft Crackdown. Reuters. 15 May 2012

Reuters reported that President Goodluck Jonathan was under pressure to prosecute top officials implicated in a $6.8 billion fuel subsidy fraud, but many of the suspects are political allies, and he is unlikely to go after them if he wishes to keep his power base. It was three weeks since the National Assembly forwarded its report detailing extraordinary corruption in a subsidized petrol importation scheme. But Jonathan was yet to indicate how he intended to react by May. Inaction on one of the biggest corruption scandals in Nigeria will hurt his political agenda and alienate his government from a disaffected population.

5. FG Lost N1.87 trillion to Pipeline Vandalism, Oil Theft: Alison-Madueke. All Africa Global Media via COMTEX. 19 May 2012

The federal government said it has lost over $12 billion to pipeline vandalism and oil theft in the last one year. The minister of petroleum resources said this at a stakeholders meeting on the rising insecurity in the sector. She explained that $5 billion was spent on pipeline repairs, while it was estimated that crude oil stolen was worth $7 billion. This was disclosed at a round-table meeting of stakeholders in the oil and gas industry, at which she decried the menace of oil theft which had become alarming in recent times.

6. EFCC Takes Over Illegal Bunkering Vessel with One Million Litres Oil. The Nation, 18 May 2012

The Economic and Financial Crimes Commission (EFCC) said it had taken possession of a suspected illegal oil bunkering vessel from the navy. The vessel was said to be holding one million litres of suspected automotive gas oil. The vessel, MT *Takoradi*, and its eleven crew members were handed over to the EFCC at Apapa, Lagos.

7. Nigerian Oil and Gas Industry Update. Crude Oil Theft Hits 180,000 bpd. The Guardian, 25 May 2012

Nigeria loses 180,000 barrels of crude oil per day to theft and pipeline vandalism, according to the Nigeria National Petroleum Corporation (NNPC). Also, the chairman of the National Task Force on Petroleum Revenue, Nuhu Ribadu, said that insecurity in Nigeria's oil and gas installations contributed to about 30 % of total loss of revenue in the sector.

Nigeria's crude oil loss has outstripped the current crude oil production capacity of Ghana, which stands at 120,000 bpd.

8. Imoke Leads Raid on Oil Bunkering Havens.
The Guardian, 26 May 2012

Ten hand-dug boats, two barges and several thousands of containers used in the illegal lifting of petroleum products in Akpabuyo and Bakassi Local Government Areas of Cross River State were set ablaze during a raid by security personnel, led by the State Governor, Liyel Imoke. About 107 tankers laden with petroleum products and pumping machines were confiscated during the raid.

9. Harmonized PIB to be Ready this Week.
Punch, 25 May 2012

The harmonized version of the long-delayed Petroleum Industry Bill, whose passage is needed to unlock millions of dollars of stalled investment into exploration and production, will be finalized this week. A copy of the 200-page PIB obtained by Reuters, included plans to partly privatize and list the Nigerian National Petroleum Corporation, to tax oil companies profit at 20 % for deep offshore and 50 % for shallow or onshore. The Senate had threatened to introduce its own version of the PIB, following delays by the executive to present a harmonized version to the National Assembly. The PIB has been years in the making, and the delays have caused uncertainty over the future of working in the country, costing the industry billions of dollars of potential investment and much-needed revenue to the government. Without the bill, analysts expect oil production to decline over the next few years. The watch dog of the oil industry, the Department of Petroleum Resources, has made a shocking discovery that only five of the approximately 20 oil-producing companies use their metering system to account for their production.

10. NNPC Short-Changed Federation Account.
   Punch, June, 2012

The House of Representative's joint committee on finance, petroleum upstream, petroleum downstream and gas resources recommended that the Nigerian National Petroleum Corporation should refund the sum of N3.08 trillion to the Federation Account, as an outcome of an investigation into how the NNPC had been remitting oil revenues into the Federation Account.

The report observed that it is the balance of the funds the NNPC did not remit to the Federation Account between 2004 and 2011. The report stated that NNPC has no right to make direct deductions from the oil revenue accruing to the federation by hiding under Sector 7 of the NNPC Act. In 2005, NNPC failed to pay a sum of $193.645 million, when it sold domestic crude at a discount of $1.211 per barrel on the 159.898 barrels of crude oil taken in that year. The loss of $193.645 dollars was then equal to N25.473 billion.

The NNPC also under-invoiced domestic crude revenue by N289 billion in 2005. Out of the total revenue of N1.45 trillion due to the Federation Account from crude oil sales, the NNPC remitted only N0.856 trillion.

It was reported that the NNPC claimed a total liability of N354 billion at the end of December 2005, which the probe said was false. Instead of claiming the sum from the federation, it was the NNPC that owed the sum of N678 billion to the Federation Account. Above that, based on NNPC's audited accounts, the nation lost about $3.675 billion through false claims by the oil companies under dubious carry agreements. The report also indicated that between 2009 and 2011, the NNPC short-changed the federation by $1.214 trillion, through unauthorized discount on domestic crude oil allocated to it. While the federation lost N67 billion through unauthorized discounts in that period, the loss through under-payment of under-invoiced value was N1.388 trillion, resulting in a total loss of N1.455 billion to the federation on domestic crude supplied to the NNPC between 2009 and

2011. According to the report, the carry agreements were the creations of the joint venture operators to confuse and create an avenue to short-change the federation. The report recommended that the four carry partners: Shell, Elf, Mobil and Chevron, who made false claims, should refund the sum of $3.675 billion. The NNPC should refund the sum of N44.932 billion which it paid to itself as cash call in 2006 alone. The NNPC should also refund the sum of $3.273 billion which should have accrued from 48 million barrels of crude oil which it concealed in 2006.

11. I Never Collected Money from Anybody Says Lawan. The Nation 11 June 2012

The chairman of the House of Representative ad hoc committee on fuel subsidy probe, Hon. Farouk Lawan, has described as baseless and cheap blackmail, media reports that a prominent member of the committee received a $600,000 bribe from an oil marketer to influence the report. Lawan categorically denied either demanding or collecting from anybody in connection with the fuel subsidy probe. He said in a situation where the committee uncovered fraud of over N1 trillion, it should be expected that the powerful cabal behind the high scale corruption in the oil sector would not only fight back, but would fight dirty. He denied ever meeting the unnamed oil marketer at the Abuja airport to receive the $600,000 first instalment of what was said to be a $3 million bribe. Lawan said he had to leave the country when the pressure became unbearable from high quarters to doctor the report to suit certain interests.

12. Ribadu: Nigeria Loses 200,000 bpd to Theft. The Nation, 11 June 2012

The chairman of the National Task Force on Petroleum Revenue, Mallam Nuhu Ribadu, said Nigeria is losing about 200,000 barrels of crude oil per day to theft. He said a new standardized metering system would soon be put in place to determine how much crude oil is being produced and sold daily. Ribadu broke the news in Abuja on June 10 during a midterm assessment of his committee's work, after a five-hour session of international oil companies and other stakeholders. According to an assistant director of the Department of Petroleum Resources, 31 of the 33 companies have been provided production metres, but only five are using the metres.

13. Oil Baron Gave Rep. 600, 000 dollars at Abuja Airport. The Nation, 11 June 2012

The $600,000 alleged bribe given to a key figure in the House of Representatives ad hoc committee on fuel subsidy probe by an oil magnate was said to have been handed over to him at the Nnamdi Azikiwe International Airport, Abuja. The money was supposed to be the first instalment of the $3 million allegedly offered to be paid by the oil magnate, ostensibly to compromise the work of the committee. Already, security agencies have retrieved the call logs of the committee member and the business man described as one of the largest donors to the campaign fund of President Goodluck Jonathan in 2011. Following the high-level of confidential data in the custody of the embattled committee member, a senior government official and some leaders of the People's Democratic Party have been talking to him to keep quiet, with a view to foreclosing a probe into the scandal.

14. Aftermath of Oil Subsidy Probe. Tension Grips Reps Over Alleged Three Million Dollar Bribery Scandal. The Nation, 11 June 2012

Barely a year into its tenure, another million dollar bribery scam is rocking the House of Representatives Ad hoc Committee on Fuel Subsidy Regime. A prominent member of the committee was alleged to have collected $600,000 from the chairman of an oil firm to influence the report of the panel which was submitted on 18 April 2012. The video of the bribe transaction may be aired on some television stations and YouTube. But a principal officer of the house said it was the prominent member who blew the lid open to security agencies by reporting an attempt by an oil baron to bribe him with $600,000. The officer said that when the vocal member from the north-west attempted to present the $600,000 publicly at the house plenary session, he was prevailed upon by the leadership of the People's Democratic Party not to do so in order not to embarrass the ruling party.

15. Reps Query diversion of N2.8 trillion from PTDF Account. Punch, 12 June 2012; The Nation, 12 June 2012

The House of Representatives Committee on Public Accounts queried the alleged diversion of over N2.8 trillion from the Petroleum Technology Development Fund. The money was said to have accrued to the account from signature bonuses but was allegedly diverted.

16. Police to Lawan: Surrender $600,000 Bribe Cash. The Nation, 12 June 2012

The police have stepped into the cash-for-clearance controversy rocking the House of Representatives. House member Farouk Lawan is accused of collecting $600,000 bribe from the businessman, Femi Otedola. The lawmaker who probed the fuel subsidy scandal insists that he reported to a house official that he got cash from the businessman who, he said, wanted his company's name removed from the list of those who collected money from the federal government, but imported no products. But Otedola maintained that he was blackmailed into parting with the cash and that he told security agents who, in fact, gave him the dollar bills that Lawan got. The police have directed Lawan to surrender the marked cash. The lawmaker insists he will not because, according to him, it is the only proof he has that he rejected a bribe from Otedola.

The Nation stumbled on some documents, including details of the interaction between the police and Lawan. In a May 9 memo to Lawan, entitled *Re: Criminal Conspiracy and Attempt to Offer gratification to Prevent the Course of Justice,* Amodu said 'Consequent upon the publication in the Leadership newspaper of Saturday 28/04/2012 captioned, "Marketers offered subsidy committee panel loads of dollars", the Inspector General of Police directed a discreet investigation into the matter'. Later in the communication between the police and Lawan, sources close to the house said that 'Lawan is prepared to lay the bride sum only before a court. He does not want his evidence tampered with'. According to the documents obtained by *The Nation*, the bribe was actually offered on April 24. Some of the documents obtained contain the transcripts of calls between Farouk and Otedola during the sitting of the committee. One memo from Farouk Lawan to the chairman of the House Committee on Drugs, Narcotics and Financial Crimes, Adams Jagaba, dated April 24, said 'you may please recall that I intimated you of the persistence of Mr. Femi Otedola, the chairman of Forte Oil, Zenon Oil and AP Petroleum, to offer monetary inducement to influence the outcome and consolidation of the report of the ad hoc committee on petroleum subsidy. In addition to the initial sum of $500,000 offered to me, was a promise of $2.5 million".

The secretary to the ad hoc committee, Mr. B.C. Emenelo, also explained his encounter with Otedola in a memo, which said I wish to inform you that I was on his invitation, at the residence of the (Zenon Oil and Gas, AP, Forte) chairman, Mr. Femi Otedola, in Maitama, (Aso Drive), this morning, and he offered me the sum one hundred thousand US dollars, in two bundles of 50,000 dollars each. The money is hereby forwarded as evidence". Sources said that, although, Lawan was tricked to collect the money, he sensed the danger and decided to alert Jagaba. The sources said that Nigerians will hear what they have never heard before on this matter.

17. Lawan: I collected 500,000 Dollars Bribe Offer.
This Day, 12 June 2012 and 15 June 2012

The chairman of the ad hoc committee monitoring the fuel subsidy, Hon. Farouk Lawan, said that he collected $620,000 from the chairman of Zenon Oil and Gas, Mr. Femi Otedola, to doctor the panel's report. Lawan, who had earlier denied that neither he nor any member of the committee collected bribe from any of the marketers, told reporters in Abuja that he actually collected $500,000 from Otedola, whom he accused of offering the money to influence the probe panel's report. The House of Representatives held a special session on June 15 on the $3 million bribery scandal and suspended the chairman of the Ad Hoc Committee Subsidy Probe Panel. In a unanimous decision, the house pledged its support for the investigation already being conducted by the police and the anti-corruption agencies.

18. Subsidy Panel in New N11 billion Bribery Scandal.
Punch, 13 June 2012

'The bribery scandal involving the chairman of the House of Representative ad-hoc committee on the fuel subsidy probe got messier'. The police have launched a new investigation into a fresh allegation that an additional 11 billion in bribes changed hands. It has been revealed that a member of the committee told the police that some members of the committee solicited bribes of N11 billion from some oil marketers. The member is said to have explained how the money was shared.

19. Tambuwal rejects plea to help retrieve $620,000 Bribe.
The Nation, 14 June 2012

The Speaker of the House of Representatives, Aminu Tambuwal, has rejected a plea by security agents to help retrieve the

$620,000 cash the businessman, Femi Otedola, gave a lawmaker. The police have asked Lawan, chairman of the ad hoc committee, which probed the multi-billion naira fuel subsidy scandals, to surrender the cash which he admitted he collected. But the lawmaker has said he will not give up the evidence that Otedola bribed him against his wish. Tambuwal rejected the request because he does not want to be roped in. He is said to be suspicious of why security agencies were mounting pressure on him to get the cash from Lawan. He turned down the request because security agencies might come up with the theory that Lawan kept the cash with Tambuwal. The speaker, being a lawyer, has enough experience to know what could happen in such a case.

20. PDP power brokers move against Tambuwal. Punch, 14 June 2012

Facts emerged in Abuja that the leadership of the Peoples Democratic Party was instrumental to the exposure of the $620,000 bribery scandal currently rocking the House of Representatives. Investigations showed that the party was aware of the bribe from the initial stage and agreed to the deal. It was gathered that the PDP was targeting the Speaker of the house, Aminu Tanbuwal, for removal, because of the belief that he was too independent for the party leaders. Sources within the top echelon of the party said that members of the committee probing the fuel subsidy met with the party's leadership and they agreed that the investigators should soft pedal on those they said were financiers of the party, who also benefited from the subsidy payment regime. The committee members were said to have been persuaded not to indict those influential members in their report. Before arriving at this, the leadership of the party had asked the committee to suspend its sitting or stop the probe entirely. When it was clear that the committee members would not allow that, because of the pressure from the public and the leadership of the house, the two parties agreed that the major oil marketers would not be indicted. It was agreed that the money should be given to the committee for logistics. It was agreed that the committee should not be hard on the major marketers in their report. The PDP was astonished when the report of the probe was released and almost everyone was indicted, contrary to the agreement between the committee and the party.

21. Rep Jagaba: I don't have $620,000 Bribe. The Nation, 20 June 2012

The chairman of the House Committee on Narcotics, Drugs and Financial Crimes, Mr. Adams Jagaba, denied having the cash involved in the bribe scandal between Otedola and Lawan. Lawan has so far refused to surrender the money. It was learnt that lawyers prefer Lawan to produce the dollar bills only at the instance of a court. A defence team source said that they were preparing for a court battle and whoever has the cash can only produce it on a court order.

22. We'll Not Discard Subsidy Probe Report Says Rep. The Nation, 20 June 2012

The House of Representatives will continue to demand the prosecution of persons indicted in the fuel subsidy probe, said the chairman of the Independent Corrupt Practices Commission Committee. He said that the bribery allegation will not lead to the cancellation of the report. The chairman, Mr. James Faleke, said that the Farouk committee did a good job and the report is accurate. He said that it is the responsibility of the anti-graft agencies to prosecute those indicted by the panel. He pointed out that the fuel subsidy probe revealed that all is not well with Nigeria and that Jonathan has not shown great leadership qualities.

23. Suspects Name Two NNPC, PDP Officials as Sponsors.
Punch, 28 June 2012

Investigators are currently probing some chieftains of the People's Democratic Party fingered as being the mastermind of the 6.5 million barrels crude oil theft.

Two officials of the NNPC and two marketers were also alleged to be part of the ring. Six new suspects, including four Filipinos and two Russians had been arrested for the theft, and six crew members of the French ship, *MT Vanessa*, used for the theft, were arrested on 21 June 2012, when the ship was impounded with the stolen oil. The suspects mentioned the names of the NNPC officials and four other ships involved in the theft ring. Two of the vessels were said to belong to two PDF chieftains.

24. Jonathan sacks NNPC GMD, Board.
The Nation, 27 June 2012

The group managing director of NNPC, Austen Oniwon, was removed as well as the oil giant's entire management board. Andrew Yakubu, an engineer, is now the group managing director. According to a statement from the president's office, the action is to further strengthen the ongoing reforms of the oil sector. Besides, the statement said the action was in furtherance of efforts to achieve greater transparency and accountability.

25. Senate Queries NNPC's Secret Account.
The Nation, 3 July 2012

Should the NNPC keep a secret crude oil foreign account? This is the knot the Senate tried to untie as the Minister of Finance spoke at a Senate Joint Committee on Petroleum (Down Stream) Appropriation and Finance. The NNPC has disowned the controversial secret account at J.P Morgan. NNPC's group executive director (finance) told the joint senate committee that the J.P. Morgan account was opened by the Central Bank of Nigeria in 2002. But the CBN had earlier told the committee that the secret account was opened and solely managed by the NNPC. The Minister of Finance had previously distanced her ministry from the account, which she told the committee they had no hand in. Also, the group managing director of NNPC, Andrew Yakubu, told the committee that the CBN owns the account. The group executive director (finance) of the NNPC insisted that the CBN is the signatory to that account and that the NNPC has no relationship with J.P. Morgan whatsoever and is not in the mandate. So who authorizes withdrawal from the account?

26. Still on Subsidy-Gate. The Nation, 9 July 2012

'There is a slew of committees probing scams in the fuel subsidy regime'. The members of the House of Representatives ad hoc committee, the Senate ad hoc committee, the Aigboje Aig-Imoukhuede Technical and Forensic Committee and the probe mandate which the petroleum minister handed to the EFCC, has been joined by President Jonathan's own presidential committee, headed again by Aig-Imoukhuede.

One wonders if the probe committee overkill is aimed purely at getting to the root of the subsidy scandal which has engaged public attention for half of the year. Or is it aimed at tiring out and confounding Nigerians so that the matter will be lost to their consciousness again. There is no doubt that the subsidy bill has run out of count The Minister of Finance, Ngozi Okonjo-Iweala has said that N1.7 trillion was paid out as at December 2011, apart from another N451 billion arrears for 2011 paid this year. Even the arrears of N451 billion is more than the N240 billion appropriated for the whole year in the 2011 budget. Already, there is clear evidence that much of the payment had nothing to do with subsidy.

27. NNPC's Insolvency Row.
Nigeria Petrochemical Report, 2012

The Nigerian Minister of State for Finance claimed in 2011 that the state-owned NNPC was technically insolvent and was unable to continue to fund its operations. The NNPC stoutly denied the claim, but admitted that government indebtedness to it was putting pressure on its operations. Reuters reported that the minister said that the NNPC owed the federation account N450 billion ($2.99 billion) in unpaid crude oil receipts, which implied that NNPC's liabilities exceeded current assets by N754 billion ($5.0 billion). The NNPC responded that it had a healthy cash flow and was able to pay for its crude oil product import obligations by using the money owed to it by the government.

The insolvency row is a direct product of the downstream environment in which four refineries with a combined capacity of 450,000 barrels per day refine less than 300,000 barrels per day. Put in perspective, it looks like some well-placed Nigerians have been saying 'let us take tap everything out this place quickly because Nigeria will soon disappear'.

This attitude has continued for five decades and it is getting more and more noticeable. It may be true that Nigeria's oil is truly a curse and not a blessing. In the latest report, a gross mismanagement of Nigeria's resources has been unveiled by the Auditor-General of the Federation. The report revealed that the account of the Nigerian National Petroleum Corporation (NNPC) is riddled with abuses. In the 2010 annual report submitted to the National Assembly recently (July 2012), the Auditor-General also observed that the Joint Venture Cash Call Account was grossly abused by the operators. For instance, an amount of $55,789,478.04 was outstanding against some foreign crude oil customers who are no longer in business with NNPC. The sum of N377,364,075.70 was outstanding against some local crude oil customers because efforts were not made to recover the debt. On the Joint Venture Cash Call Account, interest earned amounting to $1,449,047.58 was not paid into the Federation Account as oil-related revenue. Also, the sum of $200,000,000 was paid to the NNPC corporate headquarters as security payment. This expenditure was not included in the approved budget of the joint venture operations. The nature of the security, as well as the beneficiaries, was not disclosed. A loan of $250,000,000 was granted to the NNPC to fund pipeline expansion, but the debt has not been settled. There are other ugly aspects in the report, making the report the most damning revelation of how the NNPC has mismanaged Nigeria's wealth for a long time. Whether the Petroleum Industry Bill is the cure for all the ills of the sector remains to be seen.

BIBLIOGRAPHY

1. PRIMARY SOURCES

i. Archival materials/UK government documents

British Overseas Trade Board. Nigeria: Oil and Gas Export Opportunities, 1990.

British Overseas Trade Board. Oil and Gas in Nigeria. London, May 1999.

British Overseas Trade Board. Oil and Gas Reports, 2005, 2007, and 2008.

Colonial Office Files. Oil Exploration License to D'Arcy Exploration Company Ltd. And Shell Overseas Exploration Company Ltd. National Archives, London, 4 November, 1938.

Colonial Office Files. Oil Prospecting License for the Shell-BP Petroleum Development Company of Nig. Ltd. OPL No. 24. National Archives, London, 20 May, 1957.

Colonial Office Files on Nigerian Petroleum. London, National Archives, 1909.

File notes between J.S. Sadler and J.A. Davidson of Commonwealth Relations Office, London in 1960, on the proposal to establish oil refinery in Nigeria.

Letters between Anglo-Saxon Petroleum Company Ltd., Anglo-Iranian Oil Company Ltd., and Colonial Office, London. December 1936 and August 1949 on participation agreement.

Nigeria: Oil Production. Note for the Record by J.R. Williams, Department of Energy, London, 23 January, 1978.

Strategic Health Management. Principles and Guidelines for the Oil and Gas Industry. Report No. 688/307. International Association of Oil and Gas Producers. OGP Publications, UK, June 2000.

ii. Nigeria: government documents/decrees

Federation of Nigeria. *Establishment of Oil Refinery in Nigeria*. Session Paper No. 5. Federal Government Press, Lagos, 1960.

Minerals/Amendment Ordinance, 1934. Colonial Protectorate of Nigeria. Government Printer, Lagos, 8 November, 1934, Minerals (Amendment No. 3) Ordinance, 1935. Colonial Protectorate of Nigeria. Government Printer, Lagos, 5 December, 1935.

Mineral and Oil (Amendment) Ordinance, 1949. Colonial Protectorate of Nigeria. Government Printer, Lagos, 1949 Nigeria Oil and Gas report, Quarter 2, pp. 6872, 2011.

Official Gazette, No. 76. Vol. 46 of 17 December, 1959. Exploration Licence Granted under Section 3 of The Mineral Oils Ordinance (Cap. 135).

Petroleum Act 1969: Reg. 2 (1).

Petroleum (Drilling and Production Regulation), 1969.

Petroleum Profits Tax Ordinance, 1959. Government Printer, Lagos, 23 April, 1959.

Petroleum Profits Tax (Amendment) Decree No. 22, 1970. Federal Military Government, Lagos, 16 April, 1970.

Petroleum Technology Development Fund Decree No. 25, 1973. The Federal Military Government of Nigeria, Lagos, 4 June, 1973.

Petroleum Industry Bill (PIB) Inter-Agency Project. An Overview of the Petroleum Industry Bill, July 2009 (www.nnpcgroup.com/Portals/0/pdf/PIBConsultativeForum.pdf).

Privatisation and Commercialisation Decree No. 25 of 1988. Laws of the Federation of Nigeria, 1988.

Revenue Collection (No. 2) Decree, 1967. Republic of Biafra. Enugu, May 30, 1967.

iii. NGO reports

Edemhanria, I. Local Content Policy and its Implication for Nigeria. African Network for Environment and Economic Justice (ANEEJ), Benin City, 2010.

Environmental Rights Action/Friends of the Earth Nigeria. Gas flaring in Nigeria: A human rights, environmental and economic monstrosity. The Climate Justice Programme, Amsterdam, The Netherlands, 2005.

Global Integrated Oil: Nigeria, Land of Upstream Opportunities or a Thorn in the Oil Industry's Side? Berstein Research Global Wealth Management, Long View Edition, 2008, 57–64.

Oil Industry and Human Rights in the Niger Delta. Testimony of Nnimmo Bassey before US Senate Judicial Committee on Human Rights and the Law. September 24, 2008.

iv. Legal opinion papers

Adeniji, G. The Legal Framework for National Gas Utilisation in Nigeria. International Bar Association Conference, Abuja. November 27 and 28, 2000.

Legall, D. New Petroleum Industry Bill for Nigeria. International Bar Association, UK.

Local Content Development in the Oil and Gas Sector. International Law Office, Newsletter, March 6, 2009.

v. Conference papers

Egboga, E. Oil and gas and the future of Nigeria: Opportunities, challenges, roadmap to development Paper presented at the 1st Abuja Petroleum Roundtable, Transcorp Hilton Hotel, Abuja, Nigeria. March 8, 2007.

Okusami, D. An Overview of the Nigerian Local Content Act Africa Energy Week Conference, Cape Town, September 29, 2010.

Opportunities for Danish Offshore Companies within the Nigerian Oil and Gas Sector. Investment for Development (IFU) Offshore Center, Denmark, February, 2008.

Osuno, B.A. Role of the Petroleum Inspectorate Division of the NNPC as the Guardian of the Nigerian Oil Industry. Paper presented at the National Workshop on Petroleum, Lagos, 31 May, 1984.

Steyn, Phia. Oil Exploration in Colonial Nigeria. XIV International Economic Hist Congress, Session II, Helsinki, 2006.

vi. Policy papers

Cafaro, Philip J. Gluttony, Arrogance, Greed and Apathy: An Exploration of Environment Vice? The changing role of National Oil Companies in International Energy Markets. Baker Institute for Public Policy, Rice. University. Report No. 35, April 2007.

Chima, R.I., E.A. Owioduokitand R. Ogoh. *Technology Transfer and Acquisition in the Oil Sector and Government Policy in Nigeria.* A TPS Working Paper Series No. 32. Nairobi, 2002.

vii. Ph.D. thesis

Pearson, S.R. The Impact of Petroleum on the Nigerian Economy. PhD Thesis, Harvard University, Cambridge, 1968.

II. SECONDARY SOURCES

i. Books

Ajomo, M.A. Oil and Gas Law in Nigeria. In: T.O. Elias, editor. *Law and Social Change in Nigeria.* Stevens and Sons, London, 1972.

Brock, J. Analysis – Nigeria Still to be Competitive after Oil Reforms. *Reuters*, March 11, 2011.

Atsegbua, L. *Nigerian Petroleum Law.* New Era Publishers, Benin, 1993.

Ayoola-Daniels, N. *Nigerian Laws, Cases and Materials on Oil and Gas.* Petgas Global Consulting Ltd., 2008.

The World Offshore Oil and Gas Production and Forecast, 2008–2012, 2008, Douglas-Westwood Ltd., pp. 123–126.

Etikerentse, G. *Nigerian Petroleum Law.* MacMillan Publishers, Ibadan, 1985.

Gidado, M.M. *Petroleum Development Contracts with Multinational Oil Firms.* Maiduguri, Nigeria: Edlinform Services, 1999.

Joseph, Richard A *Democracy and Prebendal Politics in Nigeria.* (Cambridge, Cambridge University Press, 1987).

Khan, A. *Nigeria: The Political Economy of Oil.* Oxford University Press, Oxford, 1994.

Olisa, M.M. *Nigerian Petroleum Law and Practice*. 2nd edition, 1997.

Omoregbe, Y. *Oil and Gas Law in Nigeria*. African Book Collective, London, 2003.

Omoregbe, Y. The legal regime for petroleum production and development in Nigeria. In: C.O. Okonkwo, editor. *Contemporary Issues in Nigerian Law: Essays in Honour of Judge Bola Ajibola*. Toma Micro Publishers, Lagos, 1985.

Soyinka, W. The Open Sore of a Continent: A Personal Narrative of the Nigerian Crisis. Oxford University Press, USA, 1997.

Wikipedia. Nigerian National Petroleum Corporation. March 5, 2009.

Wikipedia. Petroleum in Nigeria. March 7, 2009.

Wragg, E. and U. Idemudia. *Corporate partnership and community development in the Nigerian oil industry*. United Nations Research Institute for Social Development (UNRISD), Geneva, 2007.

ii. Journals

Atsegbua, Lawrence. The development and acquisition of oil licences and leases in Nigeria, *OPHC Review*, 1999; 23 (1): 55–77.

Blackfriars LLP. The Nigerian Content Development. Bill: What foreign investors in the oil and gas sector should look out for, December 25, 2008; 21 (12).

Boele, R., H. Kabig and D. Wheeler. (2001). Shell, Nigeria and the Ogoni: A study in Unsustainable Development: 1. The story of Shell, Nigeria and the Ogoni people – Environment, economy, relationships: Conflict and prospects for resolution. *Sustain Dev*, 2001; 9 (2): 74–86.

Boorman, T. Hugh On Nigerian Oil. Article. *English Mineral Journal* 1909; 87: 1037.

Brock, J. Analysis – Nigeria Still to be Competitive after Oil Reforms. *Reuters*, March 11, 2011.

Clark, M., Nigeria Coming of Age. *Petroleum Economist*. Euromoney Institutional Investors Pic, London, October 2006.

Egwuenu, C.I. Nigerian petroleum laws, and regulations as they affect a commercialized NNPC. 1969; 10 (2): 8–11.

Erinne, N. John, The Nigerian gas industry offers huge challenges and potentials, *Oil and Gas Journal*, 2001; 99 (76).

Eweje, G. Environmental costs and responsibilities resulting from oil exploration in developing countries. *Journal of Business Ethics.* 2006; 69: 27–56.

Exploration and Production. *Petroleum Economist* (0306 396) 2010.

Kew, D. and D.L. Phillips. Seeking peace in the Niger Delta: Oil, natural gas, and other vital resources. *New England Journal of Public Policy* 2006; 21 (2): 154–170.

McLennan, J. and S. Williams. Deepwater Africa reaches turning point. *Oil and Gas Journal.* 2005; 103 (6): 18.

Nigeria: MEND Issues a warning. *Stratford Analysis* June 1, 2009, p. 34.

Nigerian Oil. Curse of the black gold: Hope and betrayal in the Niger Delta. *National Geographic Magazine*, February, 2007.

Odukoya, A.O. Oil and sustainable development in Nigeria: A case study of Niger Delta. *Journal of Human Ecology* 2006; 20 (4): 249–258.

Odularu, G.O. Crude oil and the Nigerian economic performance. *Oil and Gas Business*, 2008.

Ohimain, K.I. Emerging bio-ethanol projects in Nigeria: Their opportunities and challenges, *Energy Policy*, 2010; 38 (11): 7161–7168.

Omoregbe, Y. The legal framework for the production of petroleum in Nigeria. *Journal of Energy and Natural Resources Law* 1987; 5 (4).

Quinlam, M. Make-or-Break time for Nigerian oil. *Petroleum Economist*, 2010.

Smith, David N. Mineral agreements in developing countries: Structures and substance. *American Journal of International Law* 1988; 69 (560): 1501–2000.

Stohle, S.J. Nigeria set to add LPG volumes to world trade, *Oil and Gas Journal*, 2000; 98 (43): 54–61.

Ugochukwu, C. and J. Ertel. Negative impacts of oil exploration on biodiversity management in the Niger Delta area of Nigeria. *Impact Assessment and Project Appraisal* 2008; 26 (2): 139–147.

Waggoner, J. Agbami: 10 years in the making off Nigeria. *Offshore* 2008; 68 (12): 46–48.

iii. Newspapers and news magazines

Bloom, B. Bids invited for offshore Nigeria oil concessions. *Financial Times*, February 6, 1976.

Chigbo, M. Behold, a new dawn. *Newswatch*. July 20, 2009.

Fabi, R. Nigerian thieves mop up oil spills. *Reuters News*, June 15, 2010.

Cummings, C. Crude theft: A Nigerian cop cracks down on a vast black market in oil. *Wall Street Journal*, 2005: p. 41.

Kkpu, Ray. The good, the bad and the ugly in twenty-five years. *Newswatch*, Special Edition, October 1985.

Ekpu, Ray. Politics and leadership: The end justifies the means. *Newswatch*, October 1986.

Ford, N. Oil: A boom or a curse? *African Business*, October 2000.

Guest, R. Nigeria. Oil alone doesn't make you happy. *The Economist*, 2000, pp. 8–10.

Hamilton, A. Five companies get Nigerian oil concessions. *Financial Times*. July 31, 1970.

Henshall, A. 9 December 2013. Nigeria's oil-export reliability at risk, *Wall Street Journal*, 2008; 414.

HIS *Global Insight*. Oil Majors Pick Up Campaign to Modify Nigeria's Petroleum Industry Bill, November 3, 2010.

International Herald Tribune. Nigeria Plans Sales of Rights to Oil Search. February 6, 1970.

Mbamalu, Marcel. Private Refineries Lament High Cost of Licence Renewal, Ignore DPR. News Highlights, *The Guardian* (Nigeria), November 6, 2011.

Nigeria must renegotiate offshore oil contracts, says Sanusi, *The Nation*, November 22, 2011.

Nigeria Energy Market Overview. Nigeria Oil and Gas Report Q4, 2008 *Business Monitor International Ltd.*, London, 2009.

Nigeria Oil and Gas Report Q2, 3 and 4 2008. Business Monitor International Ltd., London, 2008.

Nigeria Oil and Gas Map Concessions and Licences. Latest Update. NBR Services, Paris, September, 2007.

Nigeria Petrochemicals Reports 2006–2010. Business Monitor International Ltd.

Ojomaikre, Adaighofua., Economy: Undo Jonathan's sealed failure (1) and (2), *The Guardian*, Xigeria, November 5 & 6, 2011.

Okusami D. Local content law – Is this the one? Analysis. *All Africa*, May 25, 2010.

Sahara Reporters. Wikileaks On Nigeria: Shell's Ann Pickard Says Turai, Tanimu and NNPC GMD Yar'adua Were Collecting Bribes from Oil Lifting Contracts, January 24, 2011.

Will Shell pull out of Nigeria? *African Business*, 2010, p. 362.

iv. Websites consulted

Amnesty International. Nigeria: Poverty and Violence, 2006. (web.amnesty.org/library/index/ENGAFR440172006).

Amose, K. Nigeria, Wikileaks and Moles in High Places, December 11, 2010. (eliesmith.blogspot.com/010 and elombah.com. (www.elombah.com/induex).

Brock, J. Analysis – Nigeria Still to be Competitive after Oil Reforms. *Reuters*, March 11, 2011.

Downstream Today. Shell signs deal for pipeline project. April 11, 2011. (www.downstreamtoday.com/fnf.aspx?aspxerrorpath=/news/articles.aspx).

E.O. Egbogah. Oil and Gas Sector Reforms in Nigeria: What you should know. (www.dregbogah.com/documents/69.html).

Ghazvinian, J. The curse of oil. *Virginia Quarterly Review*, 2007. (www.rqronline.org/articles/2007/winter).

Junger, S. Blood Oil, 2007. (http://www.vanityfair.com/politics/features/2007).

Media Briefing. Gas Flaring in Nigeria. Friends of the Earth, October 2004. (www.foe.co.uk/resource/media_briefing/gasflaringinnigeria.pdf).

Menas Associates. The One to Watch: Local Content online. (www.menas.no.uk/local content). March 7, 2009.

Nigeria, Oil Discovery on the Etisong Field, Offshore OML 102. oil and gas press, com. (December 23, 2008).

Nigeria to start rehabilitation of oil joint venture facilities. (www.gasandoil.com/goc/cokpany/cn951210.htm).

Nigeria Oil and Gas Online. (http://www.nigerianoil-gas.com/upstream/joint-venture-companie.htm.

Nigerian Muse. The Use and Abuse of the PTDF, June 28, 2009. (www.nigerianmuse.com/2009).

Ogunbanjo, A. An Overview of the Nigerian Oil and Gas Industry Content Development Act 2010, 2010. (www.scribd.com/doc/30564109) (Accessed on April 29, 2010).

Oil and Gas Sector Reforms: controversy rages on. (www.nigerianoilgas.com) (Accessed on March 25, 2010).

Reuters. Gas Flaring in Nigeria. Reuters. (www.uk.reuters.com/articles/2008).

The Global Oil and Gas Industry. (www.oilgasarticles.com).

Total: Nigeria: Oil Discovery on the Etisong Field, Offshore OML 102. (www.finanznachrichten.de/nachrichten-2008). March 7, 2009.

Rate this book on our website!

www.novum-publishing.co.uk

The author

He was educated in Nigeria at Ahmadu Bello University and University of Ibadan and USA at Pratt Institute Graduate School, New York and University of Pittsburg Graduate School of Public and International Affairs.

Oyeniyi has years of experience in management, university teaching, government and research.

He is an advocate of a strong relationship between purposeful development and culture. He is author of many journal articles and four books. In the course of his career he has attended several international conferences and seminars at which he presented papers. He has spent the last ten years of research and public speaking in the USA, Canada and the UK with focus on the Philosophy of Development as visiting scholar.

He writes without subject boundary, tapping from his multidisciplinary education with a touch of philosophy.

novum PUBLISHER FOR NEW AUTHORS

The publisher

> Whoever stops getting better, will in time stop being good.

This is the motto of novum publishing, and our focus is on finding new manuscripts, publishing them and offering long-term support to the authors.
Our publishing house was founded in 1997, and since then it has become THE expert for new authors and has won numerous awards.

Our editorial team will peruse each manuscript within a few weeks free of charge and without obligation.

You will find more information about
novum publishing and our books on the internet:

www.novum-publishing.co.uk